All the
Colors
We Will See

Reflections on Barriers,
Brokenness, and Finding Our Way

Patrice Gopo

AN IMPRINT OF THOMAS NELSON

Published in Nashville, Tennessee, by W Publishing Group, an imprint of Thomas Nelson.

The author is represented by Alive Literary Agency, 7680 Goddard Street, Suite 200, Colorado Springs, Colorado 80920. www.aliveliterary.com.

Thomas Nelson titles may be purchased in bulk for educational, business, fund-raising, or sales promotional use. For information, please e-mail SpecialMarkets@ThomasNelson.com.

ISBN 978-0-7852-1640-7 (eBook)

Library of Congress Cataloging-in-Publication Data [[TO COME]]
ISBN 978-0-7852-1648-3

Printed in the United States of America
18 19 20 21 22   LSC   5 4 3 2 1

For my grandmother Muriel Carpenter
Because you left your first home, this is my story.

For Nyasha
Because you left your first home, this is our story.

Contents

Part III: So Then How Do We Live?

Author's Note

Several of my essays in this collection originally appeared in other publications. In much altered formats and sometimes with different titles: "Heaven's Boxes" and "Earth's Freckled Sky" in *Not Somewhere Else But Here: A Contemporary Anthology of Women and Place*, "Washing Dishes in the Family of God" in *Relief Journal*, and "Holding On" in *Gulf Coast*. Close to as they appear now: "Marking the Color Trail" in the *Rock & Sling* blog, "Before" in *Sweet: A Literary Confection*, "Braided Love" in *Literary Mama*, and "What Remains" in *Full Grown People*. "For My Husband Driving Down a Mountain" was broadcast as a radio commentary on Charlotte, North Carolina's NPR station, WFAE 90.7. A small section of "Role Model" appeared in the *Brevity* blog.

Part I

A Starting Place

You hem me in behind and before.

—PSALM 139:5

Chapter 1

Heaven's Boxes

Before I began to read the Bible for myself, I spent many hours of my childhood curled up on the pale silver carpet of my bedroom floor, listening to a cassette player. A gentle, raspy voice told stories from the book of Genesis and spoke of worlds so far from my Alaskan home. Stories of the aftermath of creation; stories of Abram and Sarai and their journey to Canaan, of their becoming Abraham and Sarah, of God's promise that they'd have a child. I closed my eyes and imagined the woman telling the stories must look like a grandmother. If she'd been part of my church, she'd have sat in a padded rocking chair, a circle of children leaning in to listen.

While the tape deck whirled, I envisioned a great desert that reached a dark horizon dusted with shimmering stars. Camels lumbered and smelled of manure and hay. Herds of sheep bleated in the distance. I crafted tents from animal skins—so different from the tent my family used when camping beyond the outskirts of Anchorage, the backdrop of mountains climbing toward heaven, shrouded much of the year in a sheet of snow.

My mother's voice sometimes broke through the recording—her

request that I set the dinner table and her reminder that my father would be home from work soon. "It's almost finished," I would say quick enough not to miss more than a word. My mother had bought me the cassettes, and I knew she encouraged these stories of our family's faith and beliefs.

"Look toward the heavens, and count the stars," [1] God said and directed Abram's head upward. God promised descendants more numerous than the stars in the sky. So Abram left his people and his father's household. He journeyed to a land that God revealed.

My parents had mimicked Abram and Sarai. They'd left their people and their households. They'd journeyed far from Jamaica and their particular view of the heavens. They'd settled in Anchorage beneath the great North Star.

God called Abram, but the military brought my father to Alaska. He emigrated from Kingston and stopped for a few years in New York City before the army mailed him a draft notice and sent him to Anchorage. *Leave your family and the beginnings of your new American life. Leave all that behind and go.* Several years later my mother—whom my father knew from Jamaica—left her family and also moved north to Alaska.

Sometimes bits of Jamaica traveled in boxes to our Alaskan home, a variety of items my grandmother, father, or mother collected on trips to visit relatives in New York or Florida, places where Jamaicans often moved, built specialty grocery stores, and created new lives. My family filled cardboard boxes and increased their checked luggage on the return trip to Anchorage. And in our kitchen, after we'd hugged at the airport and heaved suitcases and boxes from the trunk of the car, my father sliced through brown packing tape with one quick motion, filling the room with the dry-ink scent of old newsprint. My sister and I had to wait a moment longer while my mother removed the contents wrapped in crumpled newspapers. I looked past the stories and articles from faraway places to the bounty of Jamaican curry powder, jerk seasoning, tamarind balls, beef patties, and other staples and treats. All impossible to find in Alaska.

My mother, father, and sister stacked cans of Jamaica's national fruit, ackee, on the counter and talked of heating beef patties for the next meal. I looked for the tamarind balls since they were always for me. Their tangy flavor held little appeal for the rest of my family. The sour dried fruit dusted with sugar created a sensation in my mouth reminiscent of the steam that results when water drenches a campfire—two distinct flavors coexisting in one unique form.

My family's presence in Alaska was a mixture of flavors too. Jamaican roots and an American life. While my parents adapted to mountain hikes in the frosty air and summers spent fishing for salmon, our home often featured the customs and foods from the early years of their lives—the years when they first met each other in the breezy, salt-scented air of their island home. As we lived the multi-faceted existence of Jamaican American, we were tamarind balls—not fully one flavor, not fully another, but two distinct parts coexisting in my family's unique form.

Each Sunday morning my mother brushed and combed my hair back into two braids. She slid rosettes of homemade hair bows against my scalp, and sometimes she tied satin ribbons around the base of each braid. My wide-hemmed dress billowed with the passing breeze, and I joined the other children in the Sunday school circle, my legs crossed in front of me and my mouth opened in familiar song.

> *Jesus loves the little children,*
> *All the children of the world.*
> *Red and yellow, black and white,*
> *They are precious in his sight.*

My sister and I, the little black girls in the group—we were both precious in God's sight. Precious in the sight of an unseen God who welcomed me into a circle much greater than the one I sat in each week, an unseen God who saw my differences as ordinary, an unseen God who created me.

Even as I sat with my brown skin distinct from the pale faces of others, this song made me part of the group and part of this faith. There on that giant peninsula that protruded off of the North American continent, there in that frigid place where my family found few black people like us and even fewer Jamaicans, there in that land of feathered ptarmigans and delicate forget-me-nots, I laced my hands with the hands of other children on either side. I bowed my head, closed my eyes, and I prayed.

Several years in the future, in the basement of my tiny Baptist church, my Sunday school teacher told the class about the missionary Hudson Tayler. "He left his family and traveled across the world to share Jesus with other people," she said by way of introduction. She stood near the piano and lifted a large spiral-bound book high enough for all the children to see. I stared at an illustration printed in black and white with highlights of blue. Chinese people surrounded the English man depicted with a coarse, raggedy beard. I waited with a certain eagerness to hear my teacher read from the script on the back of the picture. Hudson Taylor left his home. On other Sundays I heard how Amy Carmichael or David Livingstone left their homes too.

The children seated around me on the metal folding chairs— perhaps they thought of these Western missionaries and the homes and families they gave up because they heard God call them to China, India, and portions of the African continent. I, though, looked at the pictures of Chinese people and Indian people and black people, too, and thought of the spinning globe. Out there, across boundaries and borders, oceans and continents, existed places to live filled with people of darker hues.

And when my parents gave me an adult Bible engraved with my name for my eleventh birthday, I sat through the church service with the pages opened to the maps of the ancient world. I took my index finger and touched the possible location of Abram's Ur. I traced a path across Arabia and searched for Canaan and crossed over the Red Sea. At times my gaze paused at the scene beyond the sanctuary windows—the great spruce and slender birch trees, the mountains I knew existed in the distance beyond my current line of sight. Then I turned back to the front, raised my eyes above the heads of the people seated in their pews, and read the words on the communion table fixed at the front of the sanctuary: *Do this in remembrance of me.*

The boxes of Jamaican food that arrived in my family's home—those boxes were black and white pictures with highlights of blue. They were thick back pages of maps added as addenda to the tissue-thin pages of my Bible. They linked me to a bigger world than I knew, the world beyond my silty mud flats and inlets and my great North Star, a place where there were other types of people even if they were far away. Touching the contents of those boxes, hearing those stories of China, finding the place where Ur may have been on a map—these acts were reaching for the hands of strangers and knowing the existence of far-off places.

Chapter 2

Earth's Freckled Sky

God called Abram by a new name, and decades after my parents moved to Anchorage, I chose to alter my name. After brief seasons living in parts of Europe and Africa, I made breathless vows to a Zimbabwean man named Nyasha beneath the stretch of lavish sky. Together we chose to begin our new life in South Africa, the place where we'd met. I left Alaska and also left behind the last name I'd used for almost three decades. I compressed my life into a couple of suitcases and arrived in the shadow of Cape Town's famous mountain bearing a new name.

For those first few months, my tears arrived with a predictable regularity that left shirts unfolded and pots of rice to simmer too long on the stove. Rather than tending to the waiting tasks, I would lie on my bed with my knees pressed against my chest and my arms wrapped around my legs and sob.

Meeting Nyasha had surprised me. A mutual friend introduced us just after I arrived in Cape Town, the city I thought would be the final trip in my decade-long journey around the globe. A mixture of graduate studies and jobs had sent me to quite a few places, and after Cape Town, I just wanted to return to the Alaska I knew.

Then I met Nyasha.

"Wherever he is, that's where I want to be," I often said in the months leading up to our marriage. I spoke the words with a sort of glibness, not yet understanding the reality of wanting to reach for the one I loved but also grab hold of my home.

A month into marriage, I found out I was pregnant. Each new day I thought of the baby I now carried and the home I'd left behind. The open window brought in the scent of my neighbor's cooking, aromatic curry and other spices that reminded me of my mother's kitchen. On a clear day when I stared through the glass, I could make out the hazy shape of a purple mountain range that grazed the sky. For a split second, Cape Town would blend into Anchorage, and my new life would blend into the old.

The baby growing in my womb prompted my craving for a plate of my mother's stewed peas, a dish actually made from beans. What else could have justified my desire for a food I had never much liked before? A look of disappointment would take over my childhood face when I caught a whiff of the slow-cooked, gently spiced beans simmering away in a mixture of coconut milk and tender ham pieces. "Mom," I'd whine, "is there anything else I can eat?" In Cape Town, though, I salivated as I imagined that aroma levitating in the air. Was it really the stewed peas that I wanted? Or maybe just access to the familiar?

In the mornings, while Nyasha was at work, I walked down the hill past a large block of flats and the constant traffic around the public hospital. People moved with determined intent, and a slew of cars and buses curved around busy roads. I arrived at my local grocery store and wandered through the aisles in search of coconut milk. In the row of legumes, I tried to remember the type of red beans my mother used. A store employee in her navy-blue smock stacked cans on the shelf, but I refused to ask for help because my accent resulted in misunderstood phrases and curious stares. Once my Sunday school teacher had told me stories about people living in other parts of the world. Once I had dreamed of the faces on the other side of those Jamaica boxes. Now all I could think of were the plump memories and comforts of home.

"Mom," I said after another hesitant journey to the grocery store, my words spoken through the phone line that connected Cape Town to Anchorage. "I don't know what to do. I don't know who to make friends with. No one seems to want to be my friend. No one asks me to do things with them. No one invites me over." I sighed and continued. "I want your stewed peas. And I miss Pop Tarts." I didn't even eat Pop Tarts. How could a person miss what they didn't eat?

My mother fed me clichés. "You come from a long line of strong women. You can do this." She mentioned coconut milk then reminded me which type of beans to buy. She spoke of dashes of pepper and sprigs of dried thyme.

"Do people miss me?" I asked, and I thought of her wondering the same question many decades before. As the phone conversation continued, my mother told me about her own immigrant tears from thirty-five years ago as she explained how to prepare Jamaican foods I'd never bothered learning to cook. She spoke of continual gray in her heart despite the presence of sun and the changing seasons. Her words evoked the emptiness of snow-filled days when people's smiles hid behind the bulk of winter coats and scarves. Their lives had disappeared into the warmth of their own homes, leaving my mother standing alone in the cold. She relayed her long-ago musings that perhaps no one would really miss her if she disappeared into the white landscape. Then maybe, just maybe, she would melt away and find herself back under the blazing heat where she belonged.

"When I first came to Anchorage, the loneliness was real, but it has long passed," she concluded. Her stories gave me confidence to return to the grocery store and find the coconut milk and the package of dried beans. Later I stood at my kitchen counter and mixed together the flour and water. I kneaded the sticky dumpling dough and dropped flat circles into the bubbling stew. I added thyme and pepper in guessed quantities. Somehow the act of replicating my mother's meal spurred me to believe it time to recognize what might blossom beyond the contained world of my flat's four walls.

One evening at church, around the same time I followed my mother's instructions for preparing stewed peas, a woman named Daphne crossed the room and sat beside me. "I attend a weekly Bible study," she said. "Would you like to come?" Our lives shared little in common except perhaps our faith, our marital status, and now the invitation that settled softly between us.

In time I would discover how Daphne saw possibility in things others would ignore. She'd dye shirts that had turned yellow or stained with time or give an old desk a new existence as a pair of end tables. But that evening all I knew was that she had extended an offer to a stranger. I responded with a forceful yes. It was only the start of my second trimester, too early to feel the light flutter of confetti kicks. But I knew that with this invitation, life began to emerge.

Not long afterward, the first box arrived in the mail. Pop Tarts, Lucky Charms, taco seasoning. It felt frivolous, like a pair of gold stilettos, but I imagined taking my index finger and touching a map of the world. I tasted the artificial sweet of strawberry-filled Pop Tarts layered with sugar granules and icing. In my mind I traced a path across an ocean and a continent and rested my sight on invisible faces that saw me.

Over a cup of hot rooibos tea in Daphne's dining room, I gushed about my box of treats. And I made my mother's stewed peas for two guests.

"This is delicious," those women said, seated in my living room on my new couch. The gentle scent of a Cape Town autumn drifted through the open window, and full bowls rested in our laps. "You say it's Jamaican?" one went on to ask. "Your parents—how did they end up in Alaska?" I started a story as familiar as the taste of red beans softened in coconut milk. Over this act of communion my guests asked about me, and I asked about them. Perhaps this was how new friendships mushroomed through a veil of brittle impermanence.

Autumn moved toward winter, and my abdomen swelled as the weeks became months. I waited as women across many generations have waited to welcome babies into their homes. A cold dreariness hung across the days, but in the few hours of perfect sun, I carried a basket of wet linens down the stairs. I reached up to the clothesline and clipped clothespins over wide sheets, racing to beat the misty rain that was certain to finish the day. As I folded clean sheets or later trekked down the hill to my grocery store—as I listened to new friends talk about their children or began a conversation with a neighbor I passed in the stairwell—I found myself wondering, *What will be the journey of this child?*

On a cool evening, our bedroom lit with the yellow glow of a lamp, Nyasha spoke the name *Sekai* for the first time. Beyond the windows, night held Cape Town close, and the sky was alive with the frenzy of speckled lights. "Sekai. It means laughter," he told me. In the absence of trumpet blasts and new stars bursting into existence and the song of angels, I heard the beginnings of this baby's story, and we had a name for our child.

I gave birth to our daughter on a gray day in the final weeks of my first Cape Town winter. Clouds gathered overhead. While I couldn't confirm this, I imagined a low formation spreading across Table Mountain's plateau and a dense fog spilling down its ragged cliffs. Our daughter inhaled her first breath not on my parents' island nestled in the Caribbean Sea or my great peninsula jutting off North America. Instead, thousands of miles away, on the near tip of the African continent, the far side of my known world, our daughter began her life with the inheritance of an uprooted soul.

Months later, in the deep hours of darkness, Sekai's shrill cries pierced the stillness. Her wails startled me out of a dreamless sleep the way wails have startled mothers out of sleep since the beginning of time. I shuffled across the cold wooden floor and pulled her from the crib before further cries could seep through the thin wall and rouse our neighbors. I gathered her in my arms and sank into the chair near the window. Pale moonlight illuminated the moment, and I held my daughter close, my nose nuzzling her soft curls.

In the daylight hours, Nyasha had started to talk of leaving Cape Town. "I think it's time to go," he'd said and had mentioned the challenges of securing visas and work permits at his accounting firm. His sleeping body shifted now in the bed nearby, and I sat awake in the dark, breathing in the sweet smell of my baby.

I knew this discussion would become reality, and we would leave Cape Town. We would say goodbye to this place where fragile roots were beginning to appear. There would be other places, other cities that became other versions of home—places with terrain so flat that I would forget what it was to stare in the distance and find masses of land rising upward, covered in the mystery of low-hanging clouds.

After my two years and Nyasha's almost ten in Cape Town, we would pack our things, and I would add a box of rooibos tea in the suitcase between the folds of baby clothes and blankets. When we arrived in Charlotte, North Carolina, the city where we still live, I would unzip the suitcase and let the gentle aroma of the tea waft past my nose. As I unpacked the shoes and sweaters, I would pour steaming water over a tea bag and remember. Daphne's kitchen. My local Cape Town market. My neighbors and friends. The briskness of the unexpected winter cold.

That night my daughter burrowed her head against my chest, my husband slept nearby, and I leaned back in the chair, the room silver with a wisp of the moon's glow. Many, many years ago, I'd memorized the first verse in the Bible: "In the beginning God created the heavens and the earth."[1] I learned those words by heart long before I progressed to God pointing Abraham's gaze up at the stars. *In the beginning*, I said to myself over and over, each time remembering a God who formed something from nothing.

In the dark of an Alaskan winter, my sister and I had pulled on heavy snowsuits and completed our winter costumes with pastel moon boots and warm mittens. We had taken turns trudging up the small hill beside our home, where we flopped into plastic sleds and slid down to the driveway. Then we'd done it again and again. Up. Down. Up. Down. All the while, the stars above had twinkled against a cloudless night, and I'd seen the amber light in the kitchen where my mother prepared a warm meal.

At last we'd stopped the trudging and fallen back into mounds of snow, our heads flat against the pillow of soft flakes and the cold seeping through our damp winter clothes. We had moved our arms and legs back and forth and left behind the shape of an angel. The stars above had glimmered a radiance, distant lights that pricked the dark universe. God created both the earth I laid my head upon and the heavens that surrounded me on that frosty night.

Now leaning back in this chair with my child snug against me, I thought my head rested in a pile of snow and the sky stretched beyond the limitless width and breadth of the heavens. Different visions of the starscapes in all the places I'd ever lived, blazing reminders of what had been created by God.

Long ago I had gazed upward, my flattened body encircled by an angelic outline. On that winter night, I'd beheld a million promises that flickered across the dusky expanse of the black sky.

Part II

Formation

My frame was not hidden from you,
> when I was made in the secret place,
> when I was woven together in the depths of the earth.

Your eyes saw my unformed body;
> all the days ordained for me were written in your book
> before one of them came to be.

—Psalm 139:15–16

Chapter 3

A Theory of Known Elements

In high school chemistry, I'm taken with the idea of the periodic table. A new type of alphabet—no longer A, B, C, but now H, He, Li. A giant periodic table hangs across one of the long walls right next to the classroom window, its letters and columns and rows and atomic weights all twisting and twirling around in my mind. Sometimes I glance from the miniature table in the front cover of my textbook up to the one on the wall without the need to turn my head or look in another direction. The secrets of the periodic table are at my fingertips and in my line of sight.

My teacher stands at the chalkboard and teaches about valence electrons and how the periodic table helps us understand the ways in which elements group together and form compounds. He draws circles around the nucleus of sample atoms and speaks of electron givers and electron takers. I look back to the periodic table on the wall and scan the various elements to determine how they will react with other elements based on their placement on the chart.

There is something prophetic about this ability to stare at the columns and know that chlorine and fluorine will react with a particular element in similar ways. The more elements I add together, however, the less I know what will result. Hydrogen plus chlorine yields hydrogen chloride, but nothing I know yet can define what happens to hydrogen plus oxygen plus chlorine plus nitrogen plus sulfur. Elements are like that, predictable to a point but still with room for something unknown.

It is only later, months or maybe years in the future, that I think I am something like a chemical reaction myself, a combination of many elements producing an unpredictable result.

Element 1: Jamaica

Summer 1983. I'm not quite four years old. The planes are gone. My home is far away. The pain of my popping ears has subsided now. The crowds in the airport, speaking familiar words bent with accents I can't understand, have become a mere haze. A thick blanket of heat hangs over me, and with each breath my lungs warm. Every now and again, a welcome wind blows across my legs and arms.

The faces of uncles and aunts, cousins and family friends—all strangers to me—blend together in a stream of brown skin. More brown skin than I've ever seen in one place. People give me presents. A little teapot. Matching cups. They pick me up, pluck me from my parents' arms, and kiss my cheeks. My damp body presses against their hips.

Jamaica, my parents tell me. This is Jamaica.

Later I cling to my mother while my father stands close by. Across the long room in this new place, a man I've never met sits in a wooden armchair. My father wants me to greet him, to say hello, to speak to this man they call my grandfather. My father's footsteps creak against the floor, and he motions for me to follow, but I hide in the safety of my mother's leg. Nearby sheer curtains sway in the open window, and I inhale the slight aromas of my mother's hand lotion laced with a hint of sweat.

She touches my shoulder. The tap of my mother's fingers prods me to raise my head and peek across the expanse of the room to this stranger, this grandfather, another relative I will meet just once in my life.

Element 2: America

When I am almost five years old, I curve my body against my mother's leg again. My arms wrap around the soft fabric of her pants. The man near my mother reaches for her outstretched hand and, one by one, he rolls them across the black inkpad. Thumb, index finger, middle, ring, and pinkie, first against the pad and then against paper. One hand and then the next while the hard smell of ink floods my nose.

After the ten squares fill, the man offers my mother a tissue to wipe her hands. She gathers her purse, and I lace my fingers with hers. Perhaps, as we walk out the door, my mother mentions something about American citizenship, but this I don't remember.

Element 3: Alaska

The name *Jamaica* comes from the Arawaken word *Xaymaca*, which means "land of wood and water."[1] Sometimes I think that Alaska, where my parents raised my sister and me, could also be called by that name because it boasts more lakes than any other state in America—more than three million, leaving the runner-up so far behind that it's almost laughable.[2] An abundance of spruce and birch trees swivel toward the bluish-gray sky and cast shade across my childhood.

Alaska. The forty-ninth state. The most northern and western one in the United States—but also the most eastern, I explain to people, because the Aleutian Islands cross the International Date Line. Anchorage is approximately forty-six hundred miles from my parents' Kingston, a place that is more an idea than an actual location.

My parents choose the Anchorage hillside for our home, and we live on a quarter acre of land. A dense forest surrounds us on three sides, and each spring the melting snow floods our neighbor's yard, turning the grass, bushes, and trees into lake number three million and one. Filled with optimism, my sister and I push our sleds out on this miniscule lake, believing we can float on these improvised boats just before we sink below the surface, water rushing over the edge of our rubber boots and soaking our pant legs all the way up to the hems of our heavy coats.

In summer we run through the woods as if this is a kingdom we own or a laboratory built for our investigation of giant mushrooms or berries we collect in strips of birch bark pulled from a tree. Every now and then we slow down at the sound of snapping twigs and rustling branches, retreating at the sight of the brown fur and glossy eyes of a moose.

Element 4: Black

When I am twelve years old, my social studies teacher shows my class a movie about American slavery. He pushes the mammoth TV secured to a wheeled cart to the front of the room and shares some words about the gravity of the film. Then he switches off the long rows of fluorescent lights and twists the blinds closed.

My teacher reminds me of a middle-aged football player, tall and broad, with strands of thinning gray hair lying limp across his pale, balding head. His voice booms across the classroom as if we study our lessons in an open field or the woods near our school.

For an hour each day for the next several days, I watch the screen as people with skin like mine cower in fear and shriek in pain. Several times I listen to the whoosh of a whip flying through the air before it cracks against tender flesh. The day we finish the movie, my teacher stops me before I leave class. "I wanted to ask you a question," he says. And just as I'm the only black student in this class, I know I'm the only student he'll stop to ask his question.

"What did you think of the movie?" he asks, he face turned down in my direction. "Was it okay?"

My arms hug my three-ring binder close to my body, and I look down to the flecks of gray and brown imbedded in the white tiles of the floor. "Umm. Yeah. I guess it was okay." I take my things and escape into the hallway filling with the throng of students moving to their next class.

Element 5: Indian

One evening in high school, I pad downstairs to my father's basement office. "Interesting facts," I say to him. My tenth-grade history teacher wants each student to bring in stories about their family's history. I want more than my parents' emigration from Jamaica.

"How about our last name?" my father asks. "It's a place in India—I think an important place."

Our name? India? I think as I begin to scratch out notes. *Harduar,* pronounced as it looks except the *u* sounds more like a *w*.

My father talks for a moment about his father's ancestral ties to India. He speaks of family, generations back, migrating to Jamaica as indentured servants or laborers in the early twentieth century. And it's not just my paternal grandfather's side of my family who came from India. My maternal grandfather's side of my family did too. These two men, my two grandfathers—both Indian, both born in Jamaica, and both no longer living—remain foggy images in my memories, my child forgetfulness a mist clouding my view.

Later that week during lunchtime, I leave the voices and laughter that echo across the hallways of my high school and cross into the quiet of books. Toward the back of the library, I pull a heavy atlas from the sturdy shelves of the reference section. There, on the shabby green floor, I turn to the lengthy index and search once, twice, and then again for the place called Harduar.

That evening I share my fruitless quest with my father. "It might be with a *w* rather than a *u*," he says. "Go back and check." The next day my finger slides past several listings for Harding until I arrive at a word much like my last name. "Hardwar = Haridwar," the entry reads. Below that is the word *India*. I turn a chunk of the pages back to the map of northern India, tracing the lines of the grid, and stop at the correct square, touching a black dot labeled *Hardwar*.

I stay seated on the shabby green floor through the lunch hour, removed from the noise of the rest of the school. I remain amid the dust of reference books and the multitude of unknown things hidden from sight.

Jamaica + America + Alaska + Black + Indian ? An Unpredictable Unknown

During college in Pittsburgh, I sign up for a course called "Caribbean Culture and History," thinking that I will learn about things I want to know. After a few weeks crammed into a small room with a couple of dozen students, my professor discovers my Jamaican heritage. He mentions one or two other students in our class with connections that also tether them to these island nations.

"Will you join them on a panel for the class?" he asks.

The morning of the panel, a few of us leave the neat rows of our classmates, turn our desks around, and face the audience. Light from the morning sun pours through the window beside where I sit and introduce myself to students I already know.

"My name is Patrice, and I'm a Jamaican American. My parents immigrated to the United States before I was born." I think this may be the first time I call myself that. A Jamaican American. Not the child of Jamaican immigrants, not an American with Jamaican ancestry, but a Jamaican American.

Other students ask me questions about what it's like to be a Jamaican American. They look to me to explain something they don't know. I answer their questions. I tell them how cultures mixed in my home. I talk of spaghetti on Thursday nights and brown stew chicken every Sunday. I mention my mix tapes with a Bob Marley track followed by a Brandy track. I hear my voice tell stories of childhood, of relatives who lived so very far away. A life in a sort of in-between place. Not one side of a river, not the other, but learning how to swim in the current. I mention how I sometimes wonder what life might have been had I grown up around more Jamaican Americans. Maybe in New York City or somewhere in Florida.

A student in front of me raises her hand, "Where did you grow up?"

"Alaska," I say. The room inhales a breath, and I try to imagine what they see sitting before them. A black woman. A Jamaican American. From Alaska. Perhaps they try to mesh these elements in a certain fashion, to think how these attributes interact when placed not just side by side but combined in a way that can't be separated.

And I think about all they can't see and can't know about the depths of who I am.

"What was that like?" the student asks.

These elements formed me. Elements that hold certain properties in isolation, but that together yield something perhaps less obvious. I sit before my class, the result of a reaction of sorts. The elements combine within me, the discernable ones added to those, like my Indian grandfathers and their ancestors, who remain distant, removed, yet part of me too.

What can I understand of these elements? I wish my family—or at least others like me—were on this panel too. I long for people with authority to take my seat and call on the raised hands. But who else would have more authority about being the kind of person I am than me. Who else?

"Thank you for sharing." My professor motions to the students on the panel.

As I turn my chair back around and rejoin the rows of desks, my classmates offer a moment of genuine applause.

Chapter 4

Back Then

In the early 2000s, when I'm working at my first job and living on my own, my mother gives me stacks of found photos. Colored prints, mostly—greens, blues, browns all fading dull, with hints of yellow marking the age of the paper.

On my lunch hour, before I place the images face down on the scanner, I look hard at the young version of my mother and my father. I look at their smiles, their youth that existed before me. Sometimes I have questions: about the wedding, which was just before my mother received her nursing degree, about her hugging her family at the airport in Kingston, about her gripping a steering wheel and learning to drive on a major Anchorage road—new back then, not yet opened.

I stare so long, I convince myself I remember. Or perhaps I really can remember what I can't possibly know.

1971. Kingston, Jamaica. My Mother's Nursing School Photograph

A black and white image. You tilted slightly to the side, your face turned to the camera. You're dressed in a pressed nurse's uniform with a stiff white collar. A single stripe adorns your left sleeve, a symbol of completion of your first year of nursing school. A nurse's cap perches on top of your short black bob curving toward your chin, except for a few strands of hair flipped out to the left. These are the days when you know of Dad, but you don't yet know of the years ahead and what that will mean. A new country. A new time zone. A new home. But there remains something in your parted lips, your visible teeth, this proud and certain smile you offer the camera—as if there is unseen color in the dreams obscured by the grayscale of this photograph.

Back then, just after you finished nursing school, the intercom announced the boarding of your flight, and the sun shone sharp against a Caribbean sky. The clock face kept changing as the hands continued to turn, and your mother and little brother wrapped their arms around your shoulders and waist. They used crisp handkerchiefs to blot tears forming in the corners of their eyes. You remembered the months before, the heaving sobs from your mother, her repetitive phrase: "I will never see you again."

I think your mother pressed something into your open palm. A small memento or maybe a picture of your family. Perhaps a crocheted doily to spread across the top of the dresser drawers she believed existed in your new home. A smooth, shiny button. A shell your brother found somewhere on one of Jamaica's beaches.

Back then you knew you'd always remember the details of that day, but the mind has a way of giving in to forget. You held the heavy paper of a one-way ticket between your thumb and fingers and turned back to wave to your family. You left Kingston, knowing your new husband would greet you on the other side. Anchorage seemed like the end of your known world, and you couldn't comprehend the number of miles that formed so many time zones.

1975. Valdez, Alaska. Hiking with Dad

In the photograph you stand in the thick of an Alaskan summer, surrounded by the emerald green of shrubs and bushes and a scattering of trees in the distance. A few bursts of pink fireweed rise just behind you, and I remember my childhood hidden in the woods, collecting leaves, the occasional bunch of fireweed, the scent of an almost untouched outdoors.

Your body faces right and could brush against the sturdy stems. Your left hand could lift from where it rests against your leg and touch the petals. Your head, though, turns over your shoulder, and your tinted glasses almost conceal your eyes. Perhaps on this midafternoon hike, Dad calls your name. You twist in his direction, and Dad captures you in blue jeans, a simple white shirt, a long shadow stretching behind the two of you and beyond the frame.

I look for clues as to where your eyes land. On your husband behind the lens? On the shrubs and trees and hills I think must form the backdrop behind where he stands? Perhaps you stare past this to the expanse that widens unhindered by a viewfinder. Your nose inhales the pine and spice and clean mountain air. Still I believe somewhere lingers a wistful scent of salt, a moment when you taste humidity, when you hear somewhere, far off, waves of warm water lapping at the feet of beaches.

Back then you made lists of items to report and details to share. Every three months you held the receiver, spun the numbers on the rotary phone, and waited for an operator to connect an imaginary cord between Anchorage and your old Kingston home. How you laugh now at old stories, at the mere minutes you had, the cost of an international call. I imagine the list of things you wanted to say—the way the snow melts against your nose, the weight of a winter boot on your foot. And questions you wanted to ask: "How is everyone? How much has my little brother grown?"

I think of your brief hope that time might still. A voice, your voice, speaks calm phrases: "I'm okay. It's okay. I love you and miss you too." Your sentences must have been terse, your answers clipped. You learned how to conserve words and repeat stories with economy. I wonder if back then you thought that being an immigrant was often synonymous with missing your mother.

Months became years until years became six years, and a toddler gripped your leg, and a small baby leaned against your chest. After your long journey across the country, your mother kissed those babies she'd never met before and rubbed their curls with her open palm. By then she, too, had left Jamaica and started over in New York City— now in the same country but not the same time zone. "I thought I'd never see you again," she said once and then perhaps again and gave little thought to how her own move emulated the actions of count- less others. Your arm rested against your mother, and you touched a familiar warmth.

1979. Anchorage. The House You and Dad Built

An unfinished house blossoms from the ground, a partial frame, the rest left to the imagination. Here will be the entryway, here the steps to be covered weeks or months from now with shaggy orange carpet, keeping with the trends of the time. Next year I will learn to walk on the floors of this home. My tentative first steps will begin on the wood I see—by then layered with soft carpet covered by furniture I can reach out and cling to for balance. Boards stretch from the front of what will become the garage to the shadows at the back. At the exposed rear of the house, two-by-fours spaced equidistant apart stand ready to welcome walls. A wisp of green trees visible through the empty spaces.

You stand at the edge of the garage, your legs in the sun, your face dim in the shade. Red slacks, a blue-and-red plaid shirt. Sleeveless. Your brown arms exposed. Was Anchorage really that hot that spring? That summer? My older sister, Laurel, squishes against your hip. Her legs dangle, and her head rests just below your collarbone. She stares at the man behind the camera. Our father. You stare at your daughter, your back arched in a way that supports your growing abdomen. Me.

Light and shadows. Bits of sky visible above the stairs. "I picked the floor plan," you told me once of this house that you and Dad built together. I'm there, tucked within you, unaware of the wood, the boards, the unfinished walls, the process of creating a home. All I sense is light and shadows.

Back then you shared meals with new friends, you ate roasted turkey covered in giblet gravy at Thanksgiving and Christmas. You thought that Americans liked turkey and that holidays meant great frozen birds defrosted in sinks, roasted to a rich brown, served alongside bowls of fluffy potatoes and sweet glazed carrots. When you thought yourself ready and prepared to host a holiday meal, you took a turkey from the cave of the freezer, cooked the food, and set the table for friends. That day you discovered that not all holidays serve the same food. Now you smile at your Fourth of July mistake.

Back then friends and neighbors congregated on the tiny balcony just off the kitchen. Dad laid strips of fresh salmon on shiny sheets of foil and placed them on the grill, the hot coals beneath going from black to gray and ash. And in the kitchen with the side door partially cracked to let in the summer air, you took a platter of chopped chicken coated in the spicy pepper jerk seasoning and passed the meat to Dad. He placed each piece near the hot coals. Bowls of potato salad appeared, and a dish of baked beans too. We gathered around a table, listened to Dad speak a blessing, and we ate.

Back then you found other Jamaicans. The woman who watched me for a few hours so you could prepare for your graduation. The woman with the two young children—I can't remember how we knew her, but I remember her little girl burned herself pulling a pan from the stove. The Lukongs and Tracy. Tracy who came every Sunday and laughed with me like a big sister. Tracy who sat in the old red chair just beneath the phone and talked of her week and listened to stories and longed to eat the traditional Sunday food, dishes she'd known her whole life.

You gathered Jamaicans and others around your Sunday table, and I remember people, voices, shades of skin, the music of accents, the stories carried from other parts of the world, all served alongside aromatic grains of coconut-infused rice and chicken steeped in velvet brown gravy.

1976 or 1977. Interior Alaska. The Alaska Pipeline

There is a curve of hills and bright light from a summer sun. The pipeline enters the frame from the left and stretches back before it disappears into those hills. I can't see it, but I know that this great cylinder runs far into the distance—eight hundred miles, I'll discover one day years in the future. Tall, scraggly spruce trees border one side; a dirt road borders the other side.

My father, the only person in the photo, hiding behind the shutter of the camera, helped to build the pipeline. Really, this is Dad's picture of those summers in interior Alaska, in the heat, living in temporary camps.

Also not seen is the pregnant wife left behind in Anchorage who opens the mailbox and flips through bills to find a check and a note from her husband. Not seen is the great pot of curried chicken you make at the start of each week while Dad is gone, whittling away at the meal night after night. You reheat tender, fragrant chicken over rice, the thin yellow gravy spreading across your plate.

I've heard that taste passes from mother to unborn child. Traveling through the miniature pipeline called an umbilical cord is not just sustenance but also flavor. Now Laurel clings to things Jamaican in ways I never do. With regularity she chooses plantains from the produce section. She forms dumplings with her cupped hands.

Perhaps while Dad helped build a pipeline, you connected my sister to an even greater distance, the distance to your home.

Back then the thermostat hovered near eighty degrees in our house while snowflakes grew into drifts in yards, on the road, on the pine needle branches of trees. Inside, the sauna sensation ushered in comfort and familiarity, I assume. Now I wonder at attempts to recreate the familiar climate of Jamaica, I wonder at the silent ways people bring with them what they can't take. When other Alaskans switched off their heat for the summer, the boiler in our home continued to rumble and infused each room of our house with warm air. I never really thought about it when my friends with their pale skin left our house with bright pink cheeks after a day of play.

Back then Dad talked to the grocery-store manager and asked for special orders of rum raisin ice cream. The ring of the phone would float across the house, and we'd hear Dad say, "Thanks. I'll be there soon." In the hours of evening when I should have been getting ready to go to sleep, Dad took a pint of ice cream from the freezer, kneeled against his side of the bed, and dipped his spoon into the flavor of rum. Near where Dad leaned, old copies of the *Jamaica Gleaner* piled up alongside the *Anchorage Daily News* and *Anchorage Times*.

Back then I sat close to the *Gleaner*, special ordered to bring you and Dad connection. The pocket-sized newspaper arrived weeks late. The smudgy black ink mentioned places I'd never seen and events I now can't remember. I asked Dad for one bite of ice cream, followed by another. I tasted the smoothness, the creamy consistency, the soft raisins, the cold sliding down my throat. Across the bed you leaned back against the headboard, holding a cup of warm milk, a thin milk skin stuck to the top. You emptied your mug each night while Dad, Laurel, and I scraped the bottom of the carton.

1974. Kingston, Jamaica. The Wedding Day

A room of shadows, hints of bright rays shining elsewhere but not in this picture. Sheer white fabric covers your arms and reminds me of the curtains pulled away from the windows. A veil cascades down your hair, past your back. You sit on the side of a bed covered with a pink-hued bedspread, the headboard dark brown. A mahogany dresser stands next to you, its drawers just inches from the curve of your knee, so close you could reach out and touch the edge of a lace doily or rub the delicate silk of fake flowers in a vase. Your body faces the dresser, but your face turns to the camera.

Not Dad this time behind the lens. This, after all, is your wedding day, a day when you'll make promises that lovers for generations have been too young to understand. You smile, your hand resting on the ankle of the foot crossed over your knee. What do you know of Alaska? What can your imagination conjure up of the place? All you know is that Dad lives there and so you shall too.

I stare at the photo and indulge in familiarity. I let myself think about the wedding picture that hung in our home, the one that came down years ago when you and Dad chose to end the marriage that began this day. A marriage fractured for reasons too common to name.

I stare at the picture of a woman dressed in gauzy white. I smile with her, with you. I hope as she hopes because hope is a word shaped from textures and bold lines, a thing we can believe.

Back then a great pot of soup heated on the back of the stove each Saturday evening. Shreds of beef stew meat, Maggi soup packets with bits of noodle, dumplings dropped into the rolling broth. Despite the savory aroma, I moaned, I groaned, I pleaded. "Something else, Mom. Please something else."

I wanted spaghetti or lasagna or macaroni and cheese. "Not today," you said, and we gathered in the den—the family room, we called it—gathered around the old coffee table full of nicks and scratches and sat on the couch Laurel first pulled herself up on when learning to stand. Everyone else spooned warm soup in their mouth and laughed at the TV show in front of us while I ate cubes of beef and warm dumplings pulled from the broth. Dad slurped down one bowl and then another. And every now and then—not every week, but often enough—he told you how much he liked the soup.

Back then we'd sometimes pull out piles of old photo albums from beneath that coffee table and let the dust rise and settle around. You and Dad would point to Laurel's and my baby pictures and the shell of the house you built together. Sometimes photographs of strangers would slide from between the sticky cardboard and sheer cellophane, an indication of the album's age.

"Who's that? And who's that?" I'd ask as I tried to assign names to the faces of strangers.

"Friends we knew in Jamaica," you'd say. You used words like *Auntie* and *Uncle* with a generosity reserved for people from Jamaica but not necessarily our blood. "This is their child." I'd look at the faces of other black children scattered to places like Florida and New York, Canada and the United Kingdom too.

Everywhere but the place their parents all began.

1973. New York City. A Trip That No One Remembers

It is a time of possibility. It must be a time of possibility because your hair rounds in a large Afro that frames you like a halo. Your arms cross in front of you. A hint of a smile tickles your mouth. And those glasses with the tinted lenses stare up at me, straight in my direction, so I can just make out your eyes through the glass.

Dad is there, too, even if I can't see him. He holds the camera and asks you to turn from staring over the edge of the boat gliding up the Hudson River, turn from looking at the New York City skyline cruising out of view. "Look here, babe," I imagine him saying. You glance from the currents in the river, from the way the boat knifes through the water, and you face away from the edge. You turn toward your beloved and smile.

The people around you stand with their backs to you and hang over railings. They stare at the views, at the blue-gray water with swatches of bright sun sparkling over what divides those on the boat from the now out-of-reach city. But what I think captures you is the one out of sight. The one holding the camera, the eyes that peer through the viewfinder at your smooth, youthful skin, your dark glasses, the fullness of your hair. And through your glasses and Dad's camera lens, your eyes meet in an age of possibility when a marriage and a move to Alaska felt as simple as crossing a street.

The best feeling must be locking eyes with the one you love.

Back then we thought ourselves to be like everyone else. You. Me. Dad. Laurel. Like others we packed lunches. We folded piles of laundry and searched for missing socks. Like so many others, on

Christmas morning when we made calls across time zones, we heard the monotone message, "I'm sorry. All circuits are busy. Please try your call again later." We told each other jokes, and laughter settled across our house. Several times a week—always on Sundays—we bowed our heads, and Laurel or I repeated prayers of thanks we'd been saying for years.

We considered ourselves typical with never a thought that you— that *we*—embodied a greater story. That our presence on this mass of land, in this winter snow, in a place that grew shoots of fireweed and stems of forget-me-nots told a tale of modern migration. Here so far from a crumble of earth—an island—that broke off of a continent eons ago, here we joined with the patterns of humanity, with the way people have been moving across spaces since the first ones were cast from Eden. With our lives we mimicked those around the world, people in motion by choice and by chains, reminders of how human beings have lived as entities of movement. The small, singular moments reverberating with the way we cross the globe.

In the dark Alaskan winter, we woke in the morning and tossed heavy blankets off our bodies and bundled ourselves in snowsuits. In the summer we walked down dirt and gravel roads long after bedtime. We punched numbers on the phone and fried foods in pans of hot oils. We pulled fresh salmon from the rushing currents and wrapped our arms around each other, our bodies close. We said, "I love you." We reached out over great distances to link with others we might not even know. Together we all sat beneath an indiscriminate sun and remembered that there was something shared.

Chapter 5

Caught in the Year of O.J. Simpson and Huckleberry Finn

One morning in the thick of an Alaskan winter, when the open blinds of my tenth-grade English class brought in nothing but a blue darkness sidled with the mellow shine of parking lot lights, my teacher passed out Mark Twain's *Adventures of Huckleberry Finn*. "One of the great American stories," she said.

We spoke of the fictional characters from long ago. We discussed a plot related to slavery, related to race.

In weeks past, beyond the class door, many of these same students had joined other voices that spun through the building and settled into the walls of my high school. They repeated headlines pulled from national news, words related to a trial, again related to race. The previous summer, I had shared a couch with my mother, my grandmother, my aunt, my uncle, my sister, my cousin—still a small girl—and watched a white Bronco roll across the television screen. A helicopter swarmed in the air. Pairs of police cars trailed behind.

A face flashed across the screen. The Juice. Heisman trophy

winner. Former NFL running back. Black just like me. Everyone knew of this legend. Everyone, that is, except me. I'd never paid attention to football, so why should I know? Across the country, people tuned in to the live footage of the low-speed chase. They sat on worn couches and gripped glasses of cola clinking with ice cubes. They ordered delivery pizza, desperate not to miss how the story would end.

Now, though, copies of *Huckleberry Finn* moved across the rows and columns of desks, and I took one from the pile. A faded cover. Brittle paper. The scent of storage closets and cardboard boxes clung to the book and deposited their waxy feel on my fingertips. And here I remember Huck Finn, the mischievous hero. I remember Jim, the slave. I remember my brown skin wedged in the room of white faces. According to the frayed pages of *Huckleberry Finn*, Jim was the same color as me. I interpreted my classmates' curious stares to mean that when they read about Jim, they must be thinking about me. Even worse, though, was that word. *Nigger.* Over two hundred occurrences in that book. Each time I saw the word, I thought that this must be what it's like to sit in a puddle of dirty water.

While Huck Finn and Jim took over first-period English, details of O.J.'s trial polarized the nation. Local papers covered the jury selection process, the prosecutor, the defense attorney, the judge, and every other detail of events unfolding in a courtroom several states and a time zone away. The evening news gave updates, and the twenty-four-hour news network clamored to share details about a houseguest, about a glove, about the race card. News stories declared with some sort of national authority that one's skin color could predict one's opinion about the trial. Black America supported his innocence, and white people believed him guilty.

Maybe having skin like O.J.'s meant I should have believed him—but I didn't. At least I didn't think I believed him. Too convenient, I thought, along with everyone else around me. The motive made sense. Students at their lockers and in the hallways talked about the trial. At lunchtime they unfolded brown paper sacks and pulled sandwiches from plastic bags, speaking of O.J., his dead ex-wife, her friend. I heard the phrase "double homicide," and what lingers is the image of a black man's stoic face, his short, dark waves of hair, the deep brown of his skin, the bulk of his shoulders. I mostly listened and nodded.

When my class read passages of *Huckleberry Finn* aloud, my teacher commanded, "Read over the 'n' word. The word is offensive." My gaze dropped toward the slick surface of my desk. I remembered the first time I had heard that word—just a few years earlier, on the playground of my elementary school, near the swing set fixed against a backdrop of arctic mountains. A girl, her wispy blond hair tucked beneath the knit of a winter cap, had explained the word to a circle of children dressed in bulky snow pants and heavy coats. "That's a word for black people," she'd said, glancing in my direction. I had nodded then, too, a sign of my new understanding.

Beyond the window of my English class, in the still-dark morning hours of an Alaskan winter, I could barely see outlines of parked cars, the crowded lot, the road leading away from my high school. I watched the clock's minute hand move as if coated in molasses, as if mocking my internal pleading for the bell to chime my release. My clammy palms. My sweaty sleeves. Attempts to ignore the word only italicized and bolded it in my mind. Even what is unspoken remains, and that word referred to people like Jim, like O.J., like me. The particular shape of that string of letters, the black text printed against the off-white page.

The reminder, always, that I couldn't disappear.

When did I first learn about American slavery? Now I'm not even sure. Officially fourth grade? Maybe fifth? My parents, black though they are, weren't born in this country, and in many ways they learned American history along with me. This I remember, though: sitting in a grocery-store shopping cart and watching my mother speak with a former student who once attended the elementary school where she had worked. The grown girl, with her chin-length hair, her larger frame, her skin the same shade as my family's, mentioned the problems she was having in school with a white boy who said he wished it was the olden days so that she could be his slave.

Did I ever think O.J. might be innocent? How can I know for sure? Everyone around me nodded their heads when they spoke of his guilt. I don't remember considering the possibility of shaking mine in the opposite direction. How could I offer an opinion that might remind others how I, in fact, was not like the rest? I nodded my head. There was nothing else to do. Meanwhile, more than two hundred times, we "read over" the word that floated from the dog-eared pages to the hallway and the library, to my face, behind my back.

I had an image in my mind of the book's esteemed American author, this white man named Twain. A head full of white hair, a great handlebar moustache obscuring part of his mouth, an intense glare penetrating beyond the photograph. Years later I would learn that the book I read in high school is considered antiracist. A satirical account of the evils of the era. A story meant to make a mockery of slavery. In tenth grade I retained none of this. All I remember is the longing to finish the unit and move on.

Of course, Mark Twain knew nothing about me when he wrote *Adventures of Huckleberry Finn*. Surely he didn't intend for a black girl to squirm in her seat more than a century later. It may not have occurred to him that a black girl would ever read his book.

When the shrill sound of the bell sent my classroom into a whirl of backpacks tossed over shoulders, desk legs grating across the floor, I escaped into the flurry of hallway activity. I then rushed to the safety of algebra or chemistry. During discussions on quadratic equations or titration, no teacher's eyes ever fell on me, wanting my opinion—as if my words could somehow speak for the black experience of millions of Americans across history.

At the end of the unit, along with everyone else, I passed my copy of the novel back to the front of the classroom, turned in my final assignments, and moved on to the next classic book.

Months later, on another dark Alaskan morning near the beginning of my eleventh-grade year, I arrived at school knowing just like everyone else that a judge would soon announce O.J.'s verdict. A soft October sunrise broke into first period, and by second period daylight saturated the classrooms and hallways. Just before the eight minutes reserved for moving between second and third periods, a voice crackled across the intercom system.

"Not guilty."

A collective sigh settled over much of the building. Audible groans pulsed through the school as hordes of students began to file along to their next class. With few exceptions, the color of their skin matched the shade of the walls holding us all in. They gathered in clusters and together absorbed the news and lamented the outcome. But I said nothing, felt little but relief that this trial was over.

Two other black students walked past each other in the tight space of the hallway. The clap of palm touching palm reverberated as the girl high-fived the boy. She towered over everyone else, and her hand extended high above her like a royal scepter.

A touch of awe fluttered over me. That girl, delighting in her height, her dark skin, her belief in O.J.'s innocence. I could imagine this girl sitting in my English class and explaining to my teacher her reasons for choosing not to read *Huckleberry Finn*.

For a single moment as she passed, I wanted to catch her eye, to spread my mouth into the tentative smile one gives a stranger. A smile and nod would have gone unnoticed by those all around. Instead I glanced past this girl I'd never met, her hand high in the air. I faced the ripples of other students winding their way into a path, wanting to sweep me along. I clutched a textbook against my chest and gave in to the strength of the ever-present current.

Chapter 6

Acts of Cleaving

When I was a child, and later as a young girl, I used to scrape the remains of my dinner into the garbage can that stood in the cramped corner between our kitchen table and the side door. While carrying out this mindless act, I would often stare up at the bright canvas that hung on the wall above. The bold colors caught my attention, and with my eyes I traced the arch of the letters and the outline of two hands pressed together in a vertical position. "The family that prays together stays together," I read—sometimes aloud, more often in my head.

I gave little thought to whether I considered those words a truth. Only fifteen or twenty minutes before, I'd gathered around the kitchen table with my father, my mother, my sister, and my paternal grandmother, who lived with us. We closed our eyes, and my sister or I repeated a string of words we'd been saying for many years. "Dear Jesus, thank you for this food and bless it to our bodies. In Jesus' name, amen." A quick moment of silence pulsed around the table before we reached for serving spoons and forks and filled our plates with steaming rice, chicken, and diced carrots or peas.

On the morning of my sixteenth birthday, my parents surprised me with a bouquet of yellow roses arranged in a vase in the center of our kitchen table. My mother placed a plate of hot pancakes in front of me, the sticky syrup laced with the intense floral smell of the roses. Before I left for school that morning, my parents wrapped me in a hug and prayed for my day and the year to come.

Two years later my parents sent me another bouquet of yellow roses for my eighteenth birthday. Four and a half weeks into my first semester of college across the country in Pittsburgh, three and a half weeks before they together called me and announced the end of their marriage. I set the vase of bright flowers and baby's breath on the drab window seat upholstered in faded carpet. For several days my room held the slight fragrance of roses but failed to overwhelm the general staleness of a college dorm. Each time I looked at the flowers, I thought of sunshine—at least until the petals began to wither, the edges browning, and the rose heads drooped.

"Happy eighteenth birthday to our beautiful daughter," the words on the card read.

In the second chapter of the book of Genesis, after God puts Adam into a deep sleep, removes a rib, and crafts Eve, Adam declares that Eve is part of him. In the King James Version of the Bible, the penultimate verse of that chapter reads, "Therefore shall a man leave his father and his mother, and shall cleave unto his wife: and they shall be one flesh."[1] And sometimes I wonder if anyone takes a moment to determine which definition of *cleave* to use: "to adhere firmly and closely or loyally, and unwaveringly" or "to divide by or as if by a cutting blow. . . . to split."[2] *Cleave* and *cleave*. Two words spelled the same but with opposite meanings. Maybe some wonder, but I imagine the context makes the biblical usage obvious.

My parents navigated a long-distance relationship prior to their marriage. On an unassuming day one March, my father called my mother and suggested they marry each other that Saturday when he'd be in town. In a week my mother found a dress and planned a wedding for exactly fifty guests. "Not one more," she would tell me in years to come and mention a relative she couldn't invite because of the constraints she set. My father had a red suit tailored with such speed that the pants—or was it the jacket?—were sewn together with the wrong side of the fabric exposed.

The outcome of my parents' marriage is common. The less-than-a-week's notice is an artifact of the story I keep.

∼

Just before I started college, I came across a photograph of former vice president Al Gore's daughter, Karenna, on her wedding day. One of those celebrity magazines splashed a glossy picture of her and her new husband across the page with the information about their nuptials and her custom-made gown. Not yet eighteen, I grabbed a pair of scissors, clipped the picture, and wrote a note: "I want my wedding dress to look like this." Karenna wore a sleeveless fitted bodice and a full skirt that I knew could rise around her in a spiral of frothy fabric if she just put her legs into motion.

Years later, when Al Gore and his wife, Tipper, announced their divorce, I'd long lost the picture of Karenna's dress in the myriad moves and movement—the hallmarks of the early years of adulthood. I discovered that she had married in Washington's National Cathedral, the same place her parents had married twenty-seven years earlier.[3] I imagine she must have felt a steadiness, exchanging vows with her beloved in the same place her parents had once stood—on a day so far removed from thirteen years later when her parents would announce the splitting of their shared life.

Not long after that, Karenna announced her own separation.[4]

Sometimes I wonder what she thought as her life appeared to mimic her parents' choices. Maybe she uttered both a sigh of relief and a sigh of disbelief when her parents told her their news.

At the age of nine I participated in the first wedding I ever attended. My sister and I served as candle lighters for the wedding of a dear family friend, a woman we called Aunt even though she bore no blood relationship to my family. My sister and I wore delicate white gowns with red sashes around our waists. We carried bouquets of bright red artificial flowers set among green leaves and walked toward the altar where we lit candles arranged in the shape of a heart.

Years later when I was an adult, that same aunt's husband died of cancer. They'd found each other later in life, and they hadn't had any children. My aunt was left alone in the too-many rooms of her house. A while after that I found that old bouquet with the crumbling green foam and the fake flowers that had fallen from the arrangement. I tossed the arrangement in the trash along with other mementos from my childhood. Now I wish I'd saved the bouquet, if only to remember the formation of that marriage and the reality of a union parted by death.

$\sim$

Once, after college, I thought I loved a man. I thought I might marry him. He gave me helium balloons for my birthday, and he brought me a single long-stemmed red rose in a slender vase for Valentine's Day. On one occasion he baked chicken and rice while I sat at his round bar-height table with enough room for two people, two plates, and two wineglasses. Another time he suggested we jump into a pile of autumn leaves, a blur of gold, red, and orange rising around us as we flopped to the ground. We staggered away, laughing hard, one of my hands resting in his and the other brushing brittle leaves from my pant legs and coat.

We fought, too, over the merits of stay-at-home mothers, the question of whether children should have televisions in their bedrooms, the importance of sharing a common faith. Intangible fights about an unknown future. Subjects I can't quite recall now except for the heat that raced through me and refused to ever fully recede even after I pushed those matters aside.

"Nobody fights about these things," he told me after another normal conversation plunged into an argument.

"Nobody except us," I said.

Now I wonder if we understood how those concrete disagreements served as a stand-in for an abstract reality that two people wanted different lives. We cycled through a series of declarations that our relationship was over, followed by mournful cries of wanting someone back. I told that man that I wanted to marry for life, that I wanted to grow old with someone. He looked at me across his tall glass table with space for two and said, "That's everyone. That's not just you. That's everyone."

One summer when that man and I lived several hundred miles apart, a friend told me why she had broken off an engagement. She'd had a reoccurring dream about her wedding day—dressed in her gown, vomiting over a toilet bowl while her sister stood behind her with the sheer veil gathered in her arms, saying over and over, "Get it together. Get it together." I'd never had her dream, but I could see myself and my relationship in those nighttime visitations. Me dressed in a fitted, sleeveless bodice with a full skirt. My body hunched over a toilet bowl. A voice telling me to pull it together.

Almost two years later that man and I parted ways, severing the final fibers of us. "That's everyone," he had once said. It wasn't just me who wanted to marry for life. That was him too. So of course there could be no *us*.

~

I think I was in college when I first learned how many people love penguins. They smile and speak of how these birds pick a mate and remain with their chosen one for life. Greeting cards, commercials, old e-mail forwards paint a dream of love as two penguins united for a lifetime, spending their days together, raising their chicks together, aging with each other. We imagine a black wing lifted and resting on the feathered back of the beloved, two birds waddling together into an idyllic ice-covered horizon under a perfect South Pole sun.

In fact, though, penguin reality fails to live up to romantic fantasies. In one study of southern rockhopper penguins, the penguins only connected during mating season and spent the rest of the year hundreds of miles apart. No lazy walks on frozen beaches, wings touching and eyes gazing out at a horizon spinning together purples, pinks, and oranges. No bodies curved into each other every night while they dreamed about the future. They spend a mere twenty or thirty days together during mating season, then everyone goes their separate ways.[5]

Around the time I first encountered the myth of penguin romance, on August 31 of my freshman year of college, I heard the news that Princess Diana of England had died in a fatal car crash. A mere two years after her official divorce from Prince Charles. She was only thirty-six. The world reeled from the shock, and local newspapers printed her face on the front page for days upon days. On campus we spoke in hushed, reverent tones about the death of royalty. A week later, to perhaps less fanfare and less shock, we learned of Mother Teresa's death at the well-lived age of eighty-seven. Now I hear their names, either of their names, and I return to a Pittsburgh autumn, the way the wind rustled through my open window, the pile of textbooks and birthday cards on my college-issue desk, the sound of buses squealing to a halt and the shouts of students as they tossed a football across the lawn five stories below.

That autumn I told my parents through a phone line that snaked back to my childhood home that I couldn't talk anymore about their separation. I set down the receiver. I used my fingers to dry my cheeks and became like so many others in the world who had been wiping away tears for weeks.

I can't say what happened to the roses my parents sent me for my eighteenth birthday. Did I watch them shrivel before I carried them down the stained hallway past the laundry room where detergent freshened the air? Did I walk to the garbage can just beside the bathrooms and stare at the empty wall above the bin? For a moment did I remember the old sketch of hands pressed together and colorful words that pointed to the power of family prayers? Then did I pull the flowers from their vase—careful to avoid the thorns—before dumping the dirty water down a sink?

I like to think that I bypassed the garbage can set back against an empty wall. What I imagine is that I tied twine around the stems of the dead flowers—really, isn't the life gone out of them the moment the shears slice each rose from the bush?—and hung the fading bouquet upside down from the side of my loft bed. I want to believe that I left the birthday roses there until all the moisture drained from them, the floral aroma dissipated into the past, and I could grip a tangible memory of the original gift.

And then, when my parents called three and a half weeks after my birthday, I would like to think I heard what they said. With a single open palm, I reached to the corner of my desk to touch the fragile petals of a bouquet of dried yellow roses. I offered half a prayer, not for them but for me—an open palm that could still feel the form and shape, hope and future, of roses now gone.

Chapter 7

A Note to a College Classmate

If I could find you again, I would ask you what you remember about that day. The weight of Ellison's *Invisible Man* in our backpacks? The stuffy classroom in the basement of the old student center or the open window that provided a generous breeze? Perhaps the golden rays that flooded those who chose to sit far from the door? Could you recall the one black student—me—toward the right, slouched in a spotlight of sun?

Our instructor turned around a metal desk to face the students, the legs scraping the tiled floor. "Explain his invisibility," she said, perched at the edge of it. Wavy hair spilled down her shoulders—the same earth color as yours. The same cream complexion as yours too. Your skin matched each other, just as it matched the bodies surrounding me and the pale confines of the room.

That day the frat boys in the back saw me illuminated in the stream of natural light. "Why were the black people so angry? Why?" they asked. Their words were directed at me.

A beating of their questions. A mumble of my answers. Questions about the book? No. Questions about the days before. My blackness naked against the empty walls, and my responses summoned to speak for many.

"Disqualified," the judges had ruled after the campus relay races, when another team reported seeing our supposed false start.

"Disqualified," the judges had announced, leaving the black student group without a team. "The race video didn't show a false start, but we counted seconds. No one, no one could run that fast."

Disqualified. You were there. I was there. The frat boys, they were there too. And the black students, we moved as a unit, unflinching faces fearless in the bright sun. Our feet pounded across campus and down sidewalks edging vast, perfect lawns.

"We want justice," we said, our voices rising as one. "We want justice." Legs stepping together, arms swinging together, demands spoken together.

But in class the frat boys looked at a lone face and asked why. "Why couldn't your group just accept the judge's decision? Why?"

If I could find you again, I would ask if you saw my hands tremble. Or the way my thumb slid from the open spine of Ellison's book, letting the pages close. I think you saw my hunched shoulders from your corner seat near the door. Maybe you noticed the way my eyes darted to the clock on the wall and then settled on a blotch of floor. I know you heard the words thrown in my direction, heard our instructor sputter questions to return the class to task. Did you also hear my murmurs? Did those translate to soft cries? Is that what made you speak from the dim side of the room?

You said, "They're angry because it wasn't fair. Because it wasn't fair," you said.

I glanced to your seat and watched you turn to face the questions. Outside, robins breathed a melody, and the hum of sidewalk conversation drifted past. Roaring engines continued on their journeys. The afternoon sun still shone through the window and spilled across the world beyond the class walls. But inside my body straightened, and my shoulders rolled back as I listened to the intensity of your words.

What does it mean to sit in a golden spotlight, to be visible, and then to become seen? If I could find you again, I would look at the structure of your face and perhaps the color of your eyes. I would hold these details in the pathways of memory so you wouldn't fade to a blur. I would listen as you said your name, and I would tell myself not to forget.

If I could find you again, I would say thank you. Not because you saved me. Instead because you stepped beyond the reach of your shadow, sat in the bright light, and considered what it is to be me.

Chapter 8

Washing Dishes in the Family of God

In this missionary home in this African country that I care about and so choose not to name, I'm the one with the brown skin, and I'm the one washing the stacks of dirty plates that have been growing since last night. While I don't (particularly) think these two facts are related, it's difficult for me not to notice. *An act of service*, I chant inside my head in my friend's cousin's kitchen, which smells of coffee grounds and the sour burnt aroma of rice stuck to the bottom of a pot. *As Christ served, we serve.* I fall back on my faith and butcher a verse, welding together New Testament ideas and teachings from the Gospels. My strategy: ignore my desire to leave this kitchen behind and choose to develop a holier view.

Here in this country, my friend's cousin and the other overseas missionaries dedicate their lives to telling the local people about Christ's saving grace. As they teach in churches and run Bible studies, I attempt to reconcile my role with my appearance. My passport classification reads English teacher, but I use my teaching platform to share about Jesus.

For this year after college I'm a missionary like the rest of the expatriates I know, but I look similar to those who call this country home. At first glance, both the local people and the white missionaries mistake me for someone born here. An understandable error that I enjoy if only because, for a brief moment, I'm not alone but rather absorbed into a larger category. When I open my mouth, though, my words, my accent, my lack of fluency in the local language—these particulars all reveal the truth. So in this life—and in this kitchen too—I straddle two worlds. Not outsider. Not insider. Instead, other.

If the dishes could stare from beneath the remnants of last night's stew and this morning's cornflakes, they would focus on how I touch their gritty edges and stack them one atop the other. Or on the way I take each plate and scrape the scraps into the trash. The silverware would feel me grasp a pile, the fork tines caked with hardened rice grains and the spoons cloudy from the dried film of milk that once sloshed in breakfast bowls. Mugs with just a splash of cold coffee at the bottom wait for my touch. I think the dishes see me standing here in preparation for a thorough cleansing, in this kitchen that is far from my own.

Dishes are low on the list of priorities because of my friend's farewell party later this week and her imminent return to the States. I take in the volume of my task, the evidence of a home that overflows with visitors. I reorganize the chaos and group the dishes by categories: mugs and glasses, silverware, plates and bowls, and those obnoxious pots. The open tap fills one basin with fresh water, and I dump the mugs into the sink.

Just a few minutes earlier my friend's cousin had directed me toward the kitchen after I asked, "Is there something I can do to help?" An offer to ease the stress of a busy week and, if I'm honest, to earn my keep as a visitor in this family's house.

Ten months before, I arrived in this place of wide-branched trees with thick trunks and a bowl-shaped moon spilling over with stars, this place of winding roads disappearing into a mellow horizon. A year and a half before that, I had spent Sunday evenings in the upstairs balcony of a large church with a great steeple and walls made of stone. Over the course of several months, as the evening darkness blackened the cathedral-size windows, I witnessed a transformation of self, I witnessed crossing over a boundary. I held within my being a time of before and a time of after as I moved from subscribing to the Christian faith my parents raised me with to the other side, where I confessed with my adult words my love for—and, perhaps more importantly, my belief in—Christ.

The change may not have been detectable to an average onlooker, but I experienced a certain newness within each chamber of my beating heart. A revival of the soul, I came to think of it when I reflected later on that season of life. A sort of vividness poured itself across my world. The average trees and shrubs exploded with brilliant green. And the sky—that sacred sky. Even on cloudy, overcast, downright dreary days, I knew I saw gaps of sapphire breaking through the gray.

A harsh word from someone became an opportunity to forgive. My quick temper and impatient replies became a chance to ask my God to change my responses. I looked for opportunities to serve others, which—to me—equated with serving God. Volunteering mornings sorting used clothes. Making time to listen to people who needed to talk. Sending money to good causes. I looked for so many opportunities to serve.

"I'm giving my year after college to God," I told my family and friends. And while others began new jobs or graduate school, I delayed my first post-college job by twelve months. I packed two suitcases, boarded several planes, and arrived in the country where I now stand.

Washing dishes is an act of service, I tell myself as I reach for the knives and spoons. Particles of breakfast swish past my fingers, and slight suds begin to bubble through the lukewarm water. As Christians, we serve.

Once I watched a short cartoon of a crowd of people rushing for the best seat at the dinner table. The host motioned for the character who grabbed the best seat to give that spot to someone else. A voice spoke over the animation and alluded to Jesus' familiar words: "When someone invites you to a wedding feast, do not take the place of honor, for a person more distinguished than you may have been invited. . . . But when you are invited, take the lowest place."[1] In this home my friend's farewell party is a bit like a wedding feast. Cleaning the kitchen is akin to choosing the lowest seat.

The job is a solitary one, separated from the main traffic of the house. In the background my friend's laughter mixes with her cousin's giggles and the sound of other people who have dropped in for a visit. From the occasional phrases I catch, I know the conversation surrounds upcoming party details. I want to be there, to be part of the conversation and the planning. I remind myself that I asked to help. My thoughts whisper, *But you didn't want to be shuffled to a remote room away from all the fun.* If I were part of this family, I would leave the dishes behind. I'm not family, though, so I continue scrubbing dirty plates and flicking rice grains off heavy pots.

When I was a little girl, one of my Sunday school teachers stood before a full class and told us about the family of God. I can see her dark hair, her nodding head, her big smile. "Children," she said as her eyes traveled around the room, "when we choose to follow Jesus, we become part of God's family." I glanced around at the other boys and girls. "We become brothers and sisters in Christ." I went home and told my mother of my many brothers and sisters and how I could share my cup of juice at snack time with people who loved Jesus because they're part of my family. "Not quite family like that," my mother explained. *Not family like that*, I think now. Spiritual family, but not *actual* family.

My back prickles with the sensation of another person's presence nearby. I look over my shoulder with pleasant expectation of some conversation with my friend or her cousin. Maybe someone to dry the glasses and mugs, pack away the clean plates, and swap a few stories. But it's only the cousin's husband standing in the kitchen doorway.

Glancing at him reminds me of the day a group of us played that silly game where, one at a time, people needed to identify things they'd never done. He stood in the middle and looked around the circle. His eyes landed on me. "I've never had brown skin," he announced. He smiled at his comment, and I had to stand, give him my chair, and take his place in the center. Then there was the time I mentioned to someone that I wanted to sit in the sun. "Aren't you worried about getting too dark?" he asked when he overheard my comment. Conversations with him contained awkward references to my blackness, continuous reminders that he and I are not the same—as if this fact may have somehow escaped my notice.

"Thanks so much for the help," he starts the conversation. A safe enough beginning. Still I want to move through this small-talk exercise as fast as possible. An uncomfortable moment must wait in secret, ready to be exposed in a few minutes.

Although he has a perpetual tan the color of roasted cashews, although he has spent years church planting, teaching, and preaching in a language not his own, although he knows more about this place than I do, no one would ever confuse this man with someone from this country. His hair, his accent, and—most obviously—the color of his skin all point to a life originating in North America's colder climate. Based on comments he's made in the past, sometimes I find myself wondering whether he really supports the equality of all people as our faith proclaims and if he believes everyone is created in the image of God.

Maybe his consistent cringeworthy sentiments stem from experience working with people different from himself. Perhaps he thinks his life demonstrates cultural savvy or, even worse, racial hipness. Having lived for a good chunk of time in this African country, he possibly could imagine he's earned some kind of immunity from the pesky problems of racism.

In that same church, where I spent my Sunday evenings in that balcony populated with a smattering of people, I sang words from the book of Philippians: "May my attitude be like that of Christ."[2] I closed my eyes and opened my voice in melodic prayer. "Who made himself nothing, taking the very nature of a servant."[3] The church cleared away the chairs in the balcony for the Sunday night service, and I sat down on the rose-colored carpet in a building that smelled of a certain floral holiness. I let those words settle over my thoughts and heard only the music in the world of worship where no one else existed but me. These memories recede to remote places with the cousin's husband in the kitchen, even if he offers gratitude.

I respond to his words of thanks. "You're welcome. I wanted to help in any way I could. I'm just here to help." A half grin flashes across my face, a slight gesture that I hope will turn him back toward the hallway.

He snickers a bit, and against my better judgment I ask, "What? What's so funny?"

"Oh, just a joke. But you probably wouldn't think it was funny." His facial expression takes on a particular brightness.

"No, probably not," I say. I've taken a wrong step. I realize my mistake, but he's no longer paying attention to me. He's focused on his joke that I don't want to know, the idea that lights his eyes up with amusement.

"It's just I was thinking that you're here to help us. It's like you're our slave."

Like you're our slave. I open my mouth to respond. The words "not funny" form behind my lips, but my throat calls them back. They are true words, but they are dangerous words too. Dangerous because I'm part of the family of God, but I'm not part of this family. Dangerous because my skin color is different than his. Dangerous because some unknown force, some unseen imbalance of powers exists that enables him to speak his words while immobilizing mine.

I utter a weak, solitary, "Oh." The sound never reaches his ears, though. He exits in a cloud of chuckles. His departing footsteps clap down the yawning hallway and into the living room where his family discusses party plans.

It's a strange thing—me standing at this man's sink, passing his plates through a basin of rinse water and placing his dripping bowls in the dish drainer. It's a strange thing, even as I clean, his words want to submerge me in the dirty water, the soggy, old food catching in my hair, the dank smell rushing past my nose and soaking me through down to my toes. It's a strange thing, this man sharing my faith yet speaking as though he believes another human being is less than himself.

Does he really think this? Maybe he also lives beneath the burden of history's imbalances, even if they favor him. Perhaps his focus on skin color might reveal a misguided attempt to make light of differences and recognize the absurdity of past injustices. Maybe. But this logic fails to explain why my skin color matters more than our shared faith. Could this man and I really both be part of the same family of God?

I turn back to the work. Was this task ever an act of service? Perhaps the sense of compulsion blurred the line between choice and force.

The cousin's husband knows too well the other name for forcing someone to clean their kitchen. His comments, his jokes, his trivialization of humanity's shameful past—these acts could shackle me to this task. I could continue to scrub with a pressure at my wrists and a heaviness that reaches through my legs to my ankles. In the aftermath of his comment, I could be the one to reposition myself beneath the weight of his reality.

But with his words, I think he chains himself. He shuffles through his home with the metallic sound of clanking shackles. Could speaking the truth knock the balance of power off its fulcrum? Maybe the truth would set him free.

There is a methodical rhythm in how my hands spin and sway through the work. The right and left complement each other in the cleaning process as I swirl the diminishing stack of plates through the water and place what's now fresh on the other side. This man's words have cut me open with surprise—but not shock.

I stand in the in-between time when these thoughts of service, these predictable understandings of the first being last and the last being first begin to dribble away. What will happen in the years to come, when my mind wanders during a dull sermon or when I startle awake in the predawn hours of night, in moments like these I will return to washing and stacking those plates. I will loiter over the memory of this kitchen and dream of ten—no, of one hundred—different statements to spout in response.

None of which will alter the events of this day.

For now, though, of course I'll finish cleaning every fork, every plate, every bowl, every pot, and return each item to its proper place on the shelf. Tomorrow will be a new day. The day after that too. And on a day in the future, I will pull the plug from the sink drain and leave all that clutters the countertop behind.

Chapter 9

Becoming All of Us

When I leave Alaska and arrive at Carnegie Mellon University, I befriend the girls who look like me. We talk flat irons, hair products, and chemical relaxers that they refer to as perms. They teach me how to wrap my hair around my head at night so that when I slide my silk scarf off in the mornings, the dark strands curve in toward my face.

"P-funk" or "Patty" they nickname me in those first few weeks, and as we walk across campus to the cafeteria, they ask, "Are there many of us up there in Alaska?" They don't point at their skin, but I know what they mean. We pick at powdered scrambled eggs, push our trays aside, and reach for another bowl of Lucky Charms. For a moment I recall the many years before this when I sat in classrooms without another face like mine. "A lot less than here," I reply, which is saying something since we make up less than 5 percent of the incoming freshman class.

"Oh, you know Patty," they say when I turn up the volume on a bubble-gum pop song. "She grew up in Alaska." I sing along with the Top 40 radio station and belt out every lyric to Jewel's "You Were

Meant for Me." They poke fun at my taste in music, introduce me to K-Ci & JoJo and bring in gospel, hip hop, and R & B.

In the tired, frayed hallway outside someone's dorm room, we gather for a game of Spades, partner off, and bid on books. Big joker, little joker, deuce, deuce—I learn the new rules for a game I thought I knew how to play. I lament with my partner about losing a hand, and sometimes I even give in to the theatrics of others and throw myself down on the ground in disappointment. "We almost had it," my partner says.

"Blind six. We can do it," I say before I pick up my cards.

One of my new friends' mother tells her that we're all the same. "Really? We are?" I ask.

"Exactly alike," my friend reports back.

We laugh at the story—us black girls with shades of brown skin in the same family of hues. Us Carnegie Mellon girls toting our backpacks across campus with futures destined for greatness—at least according to the splendid brochures and college rankings we studied. Going to inorganic chemistry recitations and sitting in computer programming classes, mixing paints to smear a canvas with our self-portraits.

I list the reasons we're not the same: some of us like to go to bed early, some sleep late, others nap a solid two hours in the middle of the day. Some of us love to drink milk. Some of us get the guys, and some of us only dream. Some wear makeup. Some trek to the campus gym. And every now and then some of us skip class and walk to Schenley Park with blankets to spread over prickly grass and spend a whole afternoon sitting in the sun. Sure, we all wear turtlenecks and jeans and puffy vests too—but never the same color, of course. Not usually.

Our shirt sizes vary from small to large, but most of us can borrow each other's shoes. Then there are the khaki pants and the V-neck tops that cling to our curves. Or the thick wool pea coats, all black,

that we wrap ourselves in at the first sight and smell of the Pittsbu.
winter cold.

Because of another commitment, together we arrive twenty
minutes late on a Saturday morning for the self-defense class the campus police teach. Our instructors smile as we walk through the door.
They tell us they waited for our arrival. "No sense beginning without
all of you."

Later we giggle in our group and offer vigorous claps and cheers
when any of us raises our arm in self-defense. "Get it, girl!" we shout
in support when someone practices gouging eyes or shifts to escape a
mock predator. As we walk into the rest of our Saturday morning, we
know the campus police officers think we made teaching self-defense
almost fun.

On Valentine's Day we wear red blouses and skirts and even a
dress skimming the ground. We curl our hair and twist it up off our
faces, and we ask someone passing by to snap a picture. Or two. Or
six. We smile for the camera, but we frown when we remember the
boys who live two floors below, the way their hallway smells of stale
sweat and strong cologne, the way they hide behind old adages of boys
being boys. Those boys defaced the Black History Month posters,
they questioned the point of knowing such information, and they
started calling one of us vulgar names that won't be mentioned.

We don't remain still. We throw kicks and punches through mes-
sages sent to electronic bulletin boards and a note sent to the dean.
We call in the guys who look like us, and they show up. When our
guys storm through the hallway, those name-calling boys retreat into
their dorm rooms. Then our friends make those boys apologize. Later,
after the drama ends, the guys who look like us tell us how nice *we*
look dressed in our pretty red clothes. We smile, then waltz out of the
dorm, headed off to our Valentine's Day dinner with friends.

A few years later we all don caps and gowns, adorned with the weight of sashes and cords, medals and ribbons. We walk across stages in our clicking heels and hold our diplomas up for our families to see. Against the backdrop of bright grass and academic buildings, we pose for photographs with our arms draped across each other's shoulders. Then we disperse in different directions.

In my new city, just a few hours' drive from those Carnegie Mellon dorms and my Pittsburgh life, my white coworker jokes, "We keep Patrice around for the diversity."

A lull in conversation spreads across the table, with nothing but the sound of people chewing their sandwiches. The air smells of fresh rolls and sharp vinaigrette dressing. My food drops back to my plate, and my arms are stuck by my side.

It takes a moment, but a few of my other coworkers launch a rebuttal. One person says, "You can't say that to her."

Another says, "You should apologize to her."

To her. To her. To me.

Pink spreads over his pale face, and his expression turns to regret. "I'm sorry," he offers.

"That's okay," I reply because doesn't everyone sometimes speak words without thinking? I eat the rest of my sandwich, grab my new red coat, and walk back to my office with my hands stuffed in my pockets, alone in the terrible cold.

Years in the future, when some receive awards from their jobs and some teach college classes and some make money selling their art and some are pregnant with or raising small people, we descend on another city not too far from Pittsburgh. We arrive wearing leggings and long sweaters or tunics that could double as dresses. We walk through the city and stop at shops that give samples of heady olive oil and tangy sweet balsamic vinegar or sell scoops of specialty ice cream. At one point a white woman leans against the edge of our circle. "How do you all know each other?" she asks.

"College," we say, the same word echoing each other's response. "We met in college."

She asks where. Us brown-skinned girls. Us Carnegie Mellon girls. No. Women now.

"Carnegie Mellon," we answer.

"All of you? All of you went to Carnegie Mellon?" Her thin-rimmed glasses magnify her wide eyes. The inflection in her question falls heavy on the word *you* and on the name of our university. She must have seen the same glossy brochures and college rankings we read so long ago.

We pause, and our expressions form the beginnings of quizzical stares. One of us produces a sugar-sweet grin. "Yes," she replies.

When it's just us again, we say, "Didn't she hear us say we met in college? What do you think she meant by asking again?" We joke at her surprise. Us brown-skinned women. Us Carnegie Mellon women. We spend the rest of the weekend posing for selfies, winding our conversation through politics and old times, eating salty-sweet kettle corn and drinking lemonade with a certain laziness.

In a way, I'm back to our beginnings, back to the origins of nicknames and tragic games of Spades in our dorm hallway. Back to our khakis and V-neck tops. Back to physics, chemistry, differential equations. I walk down a sidewalk with these women in a row, and just because the statement makes us burst into laughter, we repeat the woman's words again.

"All of you?" we take turns saying, switching up our intonation from incredulous to pure comedy. At a crosswalk we chuckle as we wait for the little red hand to change. Then, in unison, my friends and I step out into the street and cross over the busy road.

Chapter 10

Notes on the Hair Spectrum

To start with, here's my definition:

hair spectrum / her 'spektrəm / noun: 1. The variety and range of hair textures or types in the world. 2. The sorting of the variety of hair types on a scale between two extremely different textures; placement on this scale may suggest differing levels of "value."

A Question

A stranger walks across the restaurant in my direction. Her skin matches my shade of medium brown, maybe a degree lighter, perhaps the color of the weak coffee that scents the room right now. Her hair lies flat against her scalp, pulled back in a low ponytail. "Your hair," she tells me, "I really like your hair."

I smile and thank her for the compliment. I reach up to my nest of curls and give them an absentminded pat. "Thanks so much," I say again.

She tells me that her hair is like mine, that now it's blown out and straightened with a flat iron, but it's just like mine. "I haven't quite figured out how to get it to curl like yours." She leans in closer, revealing a touch of bright pink lipstick on her teeth. I get the sense she wants to touch my curls, these stands twisting together in small groups, forming distinct miniature spirals. "What products do you use?" she asks.

Her expression emits a certain hope, a request that I give her something she has yet to reach, a firm belief in my outpouring of a solution. She asks for a secret to turn her hair into a head full of curls. I run through my short list of products, fairly ordinary items. Nothing too expensive or complicated.

She takes notes on a scrap of paper and purses her lips into an almost frown. She tells me how she's tried everything, an assortment of shampoos and conditioners, foams and gels that I envision piled beneath her bathroom sink.

"Maybe your hair won't curl just like this," I offer. I want her to know this may be a possibility since textures differ. Maybe I want to give her an escape from the treadmill of product searching. She shakes her head and says again that her hair is definitely just like mine. She thanks me and walks away with a bounce in her gait.

An Invention

Relaxers alter the protein structure of each strand of hair. These products use strong chemicals to penetrate the hair's cortex layer, break the disulfide bonds, and allow the cortex to stretch—all in a controlled fashion.[1] The process permanently relaxes a coiled strand and leaves behind straight in its wake. But the altered strands are weak and prone to break. And as the individual strands continue to grow, one must reapply the relaxing cream near the scalp in order to straighten the new growth.

Garrett Augustus Morgan first discovered the precursor to the modern hair relaxer in 1909 while developing a cream to reduce friction in a sewing machine. He tested his finding on dog hair before he packaged the chemicals for mass distribution.[2] "Get straight hair now," I imagine him telling black women. "Make it manageable. Say goodbye to coarse textures and coiled strands."

In 1991, my mother relaxed my hair for the first time. So began a quarterly process that became part of the next decade of my life. I used to sit in her bathroom while she parted my hair in sections, applied the acidic-smelling pink cream, and pulled on yellow rubber gloves to slick my curls into oblivion. After a certain amount of time, my scalp began to tingle and perhaps even burn. I hung my head over the bathtub while my mother used the handheld shower head to wash out the relaxer. She rinsed and rinsed until all the remnants of pink cream disappeared and the steam fogged the bathroom mirrors.

Around 1995, something went awry. The lower right quadrant of my hair fell out, black threads rushing toward the drain while my mother rinsed the chemicals burning my scalp. While this upset me, it never occurred to me to end my regular regime.

In 2001, on November 6 to be exact, I returned to my natural hair texture. With my gaze focused on the mirror in front of me, a hair stylist cut off the final processed strands and revealed an inch of curls. The first friend who saw me in the hour after my haircut said, "Oh, Patrice, what did you do?"

I hesitated a moment and tried to see myself as my friend did, my face no longer obscured by the length of my hair, a cap of short curls covering my scalp. "What I've been wanting to do for a long time," I replied. There were many reasons I rejected hair relaxers that day, but what strikes me now is the strength I discovered in those liberated curls.

A Myth

A large number of black Americans claim that somewhere in their ancestry hides a Native American relative, tucked in the branches of their lineage, covered by the leaves of the other black relatives. Perhaps grandma's mother had "those high cheekbones and that straight black hair." Perhaps it was a great aunt or a cousin on the great-grandfather's side. But somewhere in the family exists a relative who wore her hair in a long plait reaching down her back, so long and so straight that she could sit on the braid.

In his article "High Cheekbones and Straight Black Hair?" Henry Louis Gates Jr., a Harvard historian and black American, reported that, according to ancestry tests, only 19 percent of black Americans have more than 1 percent Native American ancestry. Only 5 percent have more than 2 percent. Gates says the more likely reason for those cheekbones and hair is the on average 24 percent European ancestry that each black American possesses.[3]

So why the claims to Native American heritage? Scholars Gates interviewed chalked the myth up to a variety of ideas. The way blackness has been historically treated as inferior. Lovely, though unrealistic, stories of black people and Native Americans grouping together in solidarity against a common oppressor. A desire to ignore the violent rapes of centuries past that pushed European ancestry into black bloodlines. I think some of it has to do with hair—and with a desire to say, "I'm not quite like other black people with that coarse African hair texture. I've got Cherokee in my family."

An Exhibit

Several years ago my local science museum hosted an exhibit about race. I stood in front of a wall covered in stories. Pictures of people stretched across the spectrum of human color. The gradients of race in certain Latin American countries. Another display listed an abundance of words for the many shades of brown skin.

In one story a woman shared about her Dominican mother smoothing milk into her newborn granddaughter's hair in an attempt to maintain the infant's straight strands. "Let's hope it doesn't change," the new grandmother might have said—wishing, perhaps praying, at three months and then again at six months and then again at one year that the straight might remain.

I thought of milk on an old woman's wrinkled palm, the liquid mixed with the scent of a fresh life. The Dominican Republic might be interchanged—easily—with many places. Brazil. South Africa. Jamaica. The United States. And many, many more.

A Test

During apartheid in South Africa, government officials spent countless hours concerned with the correct racial classification of individuals. They categorized people as white, Indian, coloured, or black. Sometimes classifications proved challenging when individual appearances did not suggest an obvious group. In difficult cases where the debate raged between white or coloured (multiracial) ancestry, officials would stick a pencil in the person's hair. If the pencil fell out, that person was considered white. If the pencil remained, the person had to possess some black blood somewhere.[4]

Maybe it's a rumor, but I've heard of families split in half because of the results of those pencil tests. In instances where the pencil remained tangled in someone's curls, I imagine a large stamp with the word *Coloured*, a red inkpad, and the government official's violent slam of the stamp against the inkpad and then against an individual's paper file.

The lesson being that curls are not quite good enough.

A Degree of Appropriateness

My coworker stopped me in the hallway of our office building. She touched my forearm. "It's not that I don't like your hair how it normally is," she told me. I reached up to my mane—because really that's what it was then. My mane, the curls blown out straight, a flat iron used to lock in the straight form and add a slight flip at the ends. "But you just look so much more professional with straight hair." I forced a smile before I turned and walked down the hall in the direction of my office.

A friend shares my complexion and has a head of curls coiled slightly tighter than mine. "My boss called me into her office and told me my hair was inappropriate for work," she said. "Not put together," I've heard others comment. Crazy hair. Not tame.

A white woman laughed at the irony of life. "Black women want straight hair, and white women perm their hair to make curls." I wanted to tell her that I couldn't imagine stories of white women's bosses or coworkers suggesting they add some texture to their strands in a quest for a more professional appearance. Or in the name of appropriateness.

A Commonality

A white friend told me that once she used a chemical relaxer on her brunette curls. "One of the kinds for children," she explained as she mentioned going to the store and staring at hair products in the tiny section targeted at black people. I thought of her in the aisle of Walmart or CVS—bright fluorescent lights, the fruity floral scent of hair products, and wax on tiled floors. She sifted through the different boxes of kiddie relaxers, images of little black girls with straight hair and big smiles displayed on the packaging.

The chemicals left my friend with bone-straight strands. "Beautiful," her family said. I gave her a curious stare because up until that day I'd never considered that white women might want straight hair too.

A Conversation

Another white friend—I'll call her Anna Beth—is married to a black man, and they have a son. One of Anna Beth's black friends suggested products to transform their son's mass of individual waves and curls into little ringlets, the kind that spring like tiny toy slinkies. They massaged creams and gels through his strands in attempts to coax the hair into a clear curl. The result never produced that texture often seen in advertisements, in magazines and on TV.

Anna Beth's friend asked others with multiracial backgrounds what they used and brought more products to Anna Beth's house. After several days or maybe weeks of this exercise, Anna Beth asked me what products I used. Should she be doing something differently? Did I have a secret to share? Was what they were trying to achieve even possible?

"It might not curl like that," I replied. "The individual strands might not naturally clump together and curl into distinct spirals or ringlets. That might not be how his hair works."

She didn't argue or express any sort of disbelief at my words. Her shoulders rose into a shrug.

"I think black people really like curls," I added. What I meant was *some* black people, *sometimes*. What I meant was that I've seen the desire and longing for curls in the faces of strangers who stop me at the park or in line at the grocery store.

An understanding spread across her face. Maybe her mind

traveled back in time to discussions we'd had about the straight-hair premium in society. I think she understood the way curls fit in this hierarchy. She rolled her eyes. "The thing is, he didn't care about curls until we tried to produce curls. And now he wants them."

A Truth

The shape of one's hair shaft determines the texture of a person's hair. Round yields straight hair. Oval yields curly. A flat oval yields tightly coiled.

Milk palmed into the hair cannot alter the shape of a person's hair shaft.

A chemical relaxer smoothed into the strands right at the scalp cannot alter the shape of a person's hair shaft.

The right shampoos and conditioners, gels and foams, cannot alter what a person's hair shaft produces.

A Classification

Several years ago I spent a brief amount of time exploring online forums for women with naturally curly hair. To be more specific, mostly black women flocked to the forums I frequented. Maybe curly-haired women of other ethnicities hung out together in other online spaces. But in the ones that I visited, black strangers swapped stories about shampoos to avoid, conditioners that provided the best slip for detangling curls, and the horrors of chemicals like sulfates and silicones. These women talked about taking scissors to their relaxed strands to reveal the beauty of their natural texture. They tended to identify their hair types with a combination of letters and numbers. "Proudly 4a." "Loving my 3b curls."

I later learned more about the categories. The number *2* meant wavy hair. Number *3* translated to curly hair. And the number *4* designated coiled hair. The letters served to differentiate different textures along the spectrum of a particular number. So, many women might say they grew a mixture of 3b/3c hair or a combination of 3c/4a hair.[5]

Uncertain of my letter/number combination, I perused web pages with pictures of smiling women loving their different hair textures, and I searched for the picture that best matched me. White women represented twos and maybe 3a, a Latina woman was 3b, and the rest were black women.

I pegged myself at somewhere between a 3c and 4a.

Once I read a comment from a woman who said that everyone on the forum says they are a 3c or a 4a. "Where are the 4bs and 4cs?" she wrote. "The women with those tight coiled strands, the ones where it's harder to see the curls. It's as if no one wants to be a 4b or 4c."

I wondered about the stranger's comments, wondered if these forums loved ringlet curls and skipped the tight coils, wondered if women with those textures found other places to connect.

Or maybe, as the commenter went on to add, maybe some of the 4bs and 4cs might be calling themselves by another name.

A Comparison

Many in society once referred to hair that grew from the heads of black people as wool. Evidence used by some to support the view that black people were more like animals.

A Discovery

Mythbuster Henry Louis Gates Jr. revealed results of his personal DNA testing during an episode of *African American Lives*: 50.5 percent European, 48.2 percent sub-Saharan African, and 0.8 percent Native American.[6] He expressed shock when he discovered so much white ancestry existed in his black body.

While I've never submitted samples for a DNA ancestry test, here is what I know for certain: both my mother and father had East Indian fathers and black mothers. And somewhere, tucked away in the branches and folds of my family, exists a great-great grandfather from Yorkshire, England. By this account, I find myself mathematically somewhat similar to Gates. I calculate my percentages at 50 percent South Asian (or my family's preferred colloquial term "East Indian"), 0.03 percent European, and 49.97 percent sub-Saharan African. These numbers remain my best guess given the family stories and the family evidence. I suppose I, too, might take a DNA test and uncover a rumbling of surprises and discover my 0.03 may be considerably higher.

When a friend learned about my genetic makeup, she reached into my curls, tugged them, and said that this information explained my hair.

A Reconsideration

At a store that smelled of new T-shirts and freshly printed postcards, country music pumped through the loudspeaker. As I rummaged through the dusty shelves in search of a memento of my time in that southern city—miniature guitar magnets, a postcard of downtown, a shot glass that I'd never use—I heard a woman's voice. "There, honey. My hair would look like that if I didn't relax it."

I glanced up to see a black woman and man. Her finger pointed at me, and she grinned. I wasn't sure what she meant or how to respond, if this was a compliment or a comment I shouldn't have overheard. So I returned to choosing objects and placing them back on the shelves, unable to find a suitable tangible reminder of my visit.

These many years later I remember little about the woman except her brown skin and her hair falling to her shoulders. Perhaps the feeling of being a specimen for her explanation of the need to smooth the texture of her hair into a permanent state of straight. Now, though, now I wonder if her finger pointed in my direction displayed a sort of hope. "See, honey, if I stop relaxing my hair, I'd have a head full of beautiful curls just like that woman's."

Chapter 11

Tales of Want

He sees her standing in the dim room, this woman he came back to save. A moment later, wisps of her hair touch his cheek as he draws her into a tender embrace. Soon after, this fair maiden presses her lips against his damp forehead, and the frame fills with the face of her tall, dark, and handsome hero. You roll your eyes. This movie plot is as you expected. Again the token role went to the black man, and love blossomed between him and his white lead.

Which leads you back to that summer after graduate school when you met one white woman and then another and another and another and another married to, engaged to, or dating a black man. But you didn't meet many black women married to, engaged to, or dating anyone.

"Maybe black men are the reconcilers of their race, and white women the reconcilers of their race," your white friend says, and you wonder if for a moment she has forgotten your blackness. She adds, "Black men, white women—maybe they're just more open."

You open the assigned readings in graduate school, and statistics confirm your suspicions: black men are significantly more likely than black women to marry outside of their race.

Outside of the lecture hall, your housemate tells you about the time she dated a black man. Her index finger tucks reddish-blonde hair behind her ear, and she speaks in tones so low that you have to lean close to hear. "He seemed sad, unsettled, searching," she says. She sighs about his troubled qualities. "But still he was wonderful. So wonderful."

She talks to you as if she can't tell anyone else this story. Perhaps she hopes that whispers of adoration can transform an ordinary man into a prince.

On a different day an acquaintance shares a story with you and your white friend. This woman with hair coiled just as tight as yours, and a similar complexion too, says, "The black guys at my school date the white girls, and there's no one left for the black girls to date."

How bold, you think, looking at the mixed company. She speaks of a pattern you feel too nervous to name.

During your senior year of college, you hear rumors of how the black guys piled into a dorm room and used a spreadsheet to name every black woman on your campus. Numbers populated the adjacent columns. The beautiful rankings. The desirable rankings. A scale of one to ten. Days later the spreadsheet becomes public, and you can read their thinking. High scores go to those with that light skin, with that long, straight hair.

Maybe what these black guys want is close, close, close to the fairest of them all.

"Guys love my hair," says the blonde woman across the hall from your dorm room. She speaks of the brown-skinned men she's dated, the way they like to tangle their fingers in her soft strands.

You insert occasional *oh*s and *uh-huh*s into the hallway chat because friends should listen, because it's hard to escape the conversation, because a soapbox seems too high to scale.

"It matters that black women are hard and aggressive," reads the e-mail from some anonymous white guy whose message has been forwarded and forwarded and forwarded again. You doubt that stranger even knows someone like you.

"Black women are driving off the black men," he concludes, "making them turn to white women."

A black man turns to you and a friend and shakes his head. "It's because of slave times, when masters took black women and their men couldn't fight back," he says in the safety of this same-race conversation. "Historical revenge."

Your friend pinches her eyes to slits, scrunches her eyebrows together, and brushes away his comment with a flung hand.

In high school, a friend grips your wrist, her pale fingers pressing into your flesh. Her head leans close, and her hot breath releases a whisper against your ear, "I want that. I want that so bad."

You pull your arm away and turn to glance at the brown shoulders of the guy walking past.

Down through the ages, men have crossed land and sea in search of maidens with alabaster skin. And the maidens—they stand in castles watching, waiting, ever hungry for the hand of a dark stranger.

Role Model, or Black Girls May Have Dreamed of Engineering Because of Women Like Me

In August 1997, on the first day of my freshman year of college, I crowd into a basement lecture hall with five or six dozen other students. We climb stairs in the arena-style room, fold our bodies into slightly cushioned seats, and pull fresh notebooks from our bags. A professor with tufts of white hair sprouting above both of his ears stands at the front.

I am a bright-eyed student, and this is Introduction to Chemical Engineering. When I was applying to college and searching for a major, the adults in my life reminded me that I was *meticulous, detail-oriented, thoughtful, logical*, and, of course, the evergreen phrase: *good at math and science.* So my college entrance essay sang of my desire to pursue a career in chemical engineering, which I believed to be my true fit because of my knack for balancing chemical equations and integrating polynomials.

"Welcome," the professor says from far below me, positioned near a green chalkboard. A wide grin takes over his face, and he clasps his palms together. I uncap my pen and scribble the date across the top of a blank page, ready to take notes.

∽

On an August morning in 2002, I parked my car in the visitor lot just beyond the shadow of what would become a familiar building. Slivers of later summer sunlight spilled across the concrete sidewalk outside my new place of employment. This was Eastman Kodak, the picture people, a place where young chemical engineers applied their skills to silver halide photography. Those long-gone days when many people still used film, when they snapped pictures on their cameras and took undeveloped rolls to drugstores to process prints.

I was a month away from turning twenty-three. In the days ahead I would learn about precision thin-coating technology, emulsions and dispersions, and yellow, magenta, and cyan layers of silver halide film. One afternoon during my first month, I would rise from my seat in front of my computer and leave the screen and mouse behind. I would walk down the grayish hallway with dingy tiled floors and a chain of harsh lights that magnified the faded paint on the walls. I would turn right and find respite in the women's bathroom, the walls of the room closing in on me in a way that reminded me of a thick duvet. I would lock myself inside a stall and cry with no attempts to stop the tears or wipe my face dry.

On my first day at work, though, I couldn't know that those afternoons would become a ritual. Perhaps not a daily one, but enough days that years later, when I recalled my time on the fifth floor of that industrial-looking building, I would think of the layout of that particular bathroom and the way the daylight squeaked through the opaque windows each time I sought a way to escape.

I cried not about the reality of my daily life, the commute to a seemingly endless surface parking lot, the elevator I rode up each morning, the dull walls and dusty floors. Rather, I cried about what my life might be, that there might exist another occupation replete with a greater palette of colors.

~

When I graduate with my bachelor of science in chemical engineering, I join the ranks of a miniscule group—that year black women receive less than 2 percent of the new engineering degrees in my country.[1] I wear my black robe, my cap settled at a slight angle over my dark hair. I grin wide for the department photograph. When I stare at the photograph later, I have no trouble finding myself. And no one else has trouble finding me.

On a Saturday morning in early November, a few months after I started working for Kodak, I sat with a group of children in the basement of a church. Turquoise-gray padded seats fanned out in rows across the room, reminiscent of the shape and structure of my college lecture halls, recalling the way I once found my spot and stared at the front. Children surrounded me, interspersed with an occasional adult leader. The director of the urban ministry motioned me to the stage. He stood in jeans and a navy-blue sweatshirt, a button with a picture of his wife's smiling face pinned near his left sleeve. A pianist and a few vocalists hovered in the background.

"This is Miss Patrice," the director said to the audience of children and leaders, and he asked me to tell everyone something about myself. Outside the building the air grew chilly with the onset of the Rochester winter—colder temperatures but no snow quite yet. Inside I was warm and beginning to sweat beneath the stares of so many. I'd been at this church only a few weeks, but I had thought, perhaps, among these children and the rest of these leaders, I might find a temporary home.

"I'm Miss Patrice, and I've been living in Rochester since August. I work at Kodak as a chemical engineer." The ministry director took a step back and gave me and my story several approving nods.

"Did you hear that everyone? She said she's an engineer. She went to college, and she became an engineer."

A few years after my college graduation, I leave the field of chemical engineering and decide to attend graduate school. I spend some time pursuing a career in community development before I finally stumble into writing. At a writing conference in the same city where I studied chemical engineering, my workshop leader suggests the class all go to lunch together so we can talk some more about writing.

We leave the conference venue and walk through the heat of a late spring day, down familiar sidewalks, passing the same stone apartment building where I lived during my senior year of college. We gather around two square tables pushed together at a noodle house I frequented after late-night study sessions.

Somewhere in the conversation, after placing our order and before the plates of noodles and dumplings arrive—smelling the same tangy and savory scent I remember—my past as an engineer surfaces. A chemical engineer, I explain to everyone. They give me several questioning expressions, wondering how an engineer became a writer.

"I loved writing," I say, "but I was good at math and science.

People really like girls who are good at math and science to pursue engineering."

My workshop leader replies, "Become an engineer not just for you but for all the other women."

"Not just for all the other women," I say, "but for all the other black women." As if by my choosing that degree, women like me could unravel history and make up for paths once closed.

During National Engineering Week that first February I worked for Kodak, I traveled with coworkers to a local middle school. I stood behind a pressed wood and metal folding table placed in one corner of the intersection of two hallways. Three more matching tables stood in every other corner of the space.

The children filed past me in clumps of five or six and paused near my table before moving on to the next. I'd never walked the halls of this school, picked at nachos in the cafeteria, or rushed through a math assignment outside of homeroom. Until this day, I'd never been inside this building as a student or teacher or member of this community. Occasionally I glanced at a girl in a bright shirt, backpack hanging from her shoulders, or another with an open notebook and her hair pulled into braids, and I glimpsed a soft and subtle familiarity of the child I remembered myself being.

"Miss Patrice!" I heard a voice call in the middle of my mini lesson about image science and engineering. Coming toward my table was a girl I spent Saturday mornings with in the basement of my church. She wore an oversized sweatshirt and an inkling of a smile, her black curls slicked back into a side ponytail. The girl grabbed her friends and pulled them over to my table. I gave them magenta, cyan, and yellow light filters and showed them how to sift one over the other and form red, green, and blue.

91

~

My friend Sayiwe, another former engineer, asks me if I want to see the movie *Hidden Figures* with her and her friend. "A girls' night," she says in her text message. I've known Sayiwe a long time, our years reaching back to our college days when we both studied engineering.

That Sunday night we climb the stairs of the darkened theater, find our assigned seats, and sink into the plush chairs. For two hours I imagine what I might have been at another place and another time. When Taraji P. Henson playing Katherine Johnson pounds out an equation across a chalkboard and reaches a solution, I emit an audible sigh. I recall a deep breath I once took back in Introduction to Chemical Engineering when I solved a mass balance for strawberry jam production.

When we rise from our seats after the eerie yellow lights come on, after the credits end, and after the bulk of the theater's crowd disappears into the hallway, I say to Sayiwe, "It makes me wish I still worked as an engineer."

"Me too," she says.

There was a power portrayed on the screen, a power I'm not sure I'd ever latched on to before, a power perhaps always there. Within the equations of my old textbooks, within the memories of understanding the law of thermodynamics and reaction engineering—within these places lies abundance, an abundance maybe too great for me to notice. Wondrous moments when you press forth into the unknown, whether in the smallness of a simple strawberry jam mass balance or the grandiose, audacious dream of propelling a human being into space. You press forth into the unknown, and the other side, the reality of the other side, pierces your heart in a way that reminds you of your humanness, of your possibilities, of your very life.

A report mentions that one reason for the absence of black women engineering students is the lack of black women engineers, the lack of examples a few steps ahead to help them envision their future.[2]

Once a young girl called, "Miss Patrice," across the hallway. She and her friends stood before me as I taught them about the properties of light. They took filters and placed them one over the other, revealing a world of color they couldn't have imagined.

As I watched on a movie screen the portrayal of a woman who looked like me isolate variables and solve complex math equations, an electric surge ripped through me. And I think, in a microscopic way, those girls experienced a similar surge, a jolt of knowing and understanding. In the hallway, they tasted the burst of euphoria that comes from expansion of the mind.

The end was inevitable, the exact time not so certain. Those calculus problems and chemical reactions had brought me to a comfortable, firm and steady, predictably certain trance, one that aligned well with exact definitions, right answers, periodic tables, and known expectations for left-brained degrees. But what I longed for was a sky split open, to become a scholar of more.

The engineering, the distillation columns, the steam tables, these were only beginnings, places where one dips in a toe and tests the water. For a moment there is a twinkle of recognition, a whisper of familiarity. Then the haze passes, the clouds separate. And what became clear for me was that *here* was not the place, but *here* carried with it the precise weight of inexplicable richness.

And so what I want to say to the little girls I once tutored while I was in college and to the ones who sat with me in the basement of a church and the ones who stopped at my table and listened to me explain the primary colors of light. To them and the young ones who nodded their heads when I compared engineering to baking cookies and finding a way to make cookies not just for their families but for a whole city. To those girls who looked at me, looked at my complexion, and saw a picture of what they could become. And maybe even more so to the girls who never saw me, heard me, and thus never imagined.

To all of you, what I want to say is, I'm sorry I left. I'm sorry I didn't stay.

I was born into this particular moment in time in this particular place. Not forty years before or four hundred years before. Not forty years after or four hundred years after. But now. And at this particular moment in time, in this particular place, for women and girls like me, I recognize my pursuits as not divorced from the eyes of others looking for an example of what they might become.

But now I wonder if perhaps searching for a sky split open was never about leaving or remaining. Maybe it was always about embracing the ability to change and transform, to flourish with the fullness of the freedom to pursue something more.

So if I'm sorry I left, then I must also be thankful I didn't stay.

Many years after I cease referring to myself as a chemical engineer, I haul sagging boxes into my living room with plans to sort through the contents. I delve into the decades of my past, dividing the previous periods of my life into clumsy piles of what to keep and what to throw away. Tattered case studies from graduate school. A piece of dull metal I melted and poured during an engineering lab my freshman year of college. A commencement program tucked beneath the sash I wore with my graduation robe.

At the bottom of one box, I find an old textbook, brick red in color, *Elementary Principles of Chemical Processes* written in capital letters down the spine. I run my fingers across the indentation of letters, open the front cover, and find my own notes about the density of water written in my long-ago, still familiar script. I drift back to the basement lecture hall and the first day of college, to folding myself into a chair and scribbling the date across a fresh sheet of paper. I pause at the end-of-chapter problem and form a mental process for working a solution before I set the textbook in the pile of what will stay.

Later I place the textbook on the shelf with my literary journals and essays collections, squeezed next to books about the craft of writing. I leave this brick-red bit of personal history to gather a fine layer of dust until the next time I pull the book from the shelf, turn the pages, and remember all that I have been and all that I am and all that I am becoming.

Chapter 13

On Degrees of Blackness
and Being Me

"I don't really think of you as being black," a dear college friend once said to me when we were much younger and both prone to verbalizing our internal thoughts without giving much consideration to the impact of our words. Now I've forgotten the topic of that phone discussion or what triggered the formation of her comment. I imagine she had relayed a personal story of being a black child in a mostly white elementary school. In turn I shared my version of a similar experience. After hearing my story, she may have said something like, "I'm always surprised when you say these things," followed by her statement that classified me as not being black like her.

I held the phone against my ear and paused a moment as mild indignation crept through my mind. "Of course I'm black," I replied. I moved on to other topics, brushing past her words, and much later, after we'd exhausted all the rambling discussions good friends have, I returned my phone to its cradle on the counter. Only later that night and even years into the future, in the midst of mindless

activity—driving down the highway, heating leftovers for dinner—
did I dwell again on her comment. If there was a circle of blackness I
could be part of, her statement made my membership uncertain in my
friend's eyes, a person I had no doubt fit firmly within the definition
of being black. I stood at the edge of a porous border with a grasp
that was tenuous at best. How black could I be if even my dear friend
questioned my blackness?

While the context for the conversation and my friend's memory
of the incident have been washed away, the words remain in my mind,
the short phrase exacting a sort of power over me. I asked her in an
e-mail whether she remembered the incident. "Even if you've forgotten, can you guess what might have prompted you to think that way?"
I offered her a multiple-choice questionnaire. "Here are some potential options," I explained.

1.   My Jamaican parents/family. My parents immigrated to the
United States as young adults. The history of being black in America
was not the history they grew up with. I offered my friend what I
thought to be an elegant solution—that to be black meant more than
the color of your skin.

2.   My multiracial heritage. To the casual nonblack observer, it's
easy to classify me in the category of black or African American. "Are
you mixed," a black friend asked me once shortly after we'd met, a
question repeated by many other black people over the years. Two
black Jamaican grandmothers, two Indian—East Indian they were
called in Jamaica—grandfathers. I knew this heritage in a way might
reduce my blackness by about half.

3.   My Alaskan childhood. "There goes random black boy,"
my college friends and I used to whisper to each other as we passed
certain black guys walking across campus. There were random black
girls too—the students who had brown skin like us but who showed
little interest in connecting with the other black students, remaining

entrenched in mostly white communities. "They don't know about being black," we'd discuss over pizza at the student union when one of them walked past and didn't even glance in our direction. I spent my childhood in a white community. Before I met my black friends in college, I spent my high school days in Alaska being "random black girl" to the trickling of other black students in my school. Perhaps even having a history as a "random black girl" impacted my level of blackness in the present day.

4. My historic lack of familiarity with certain ideas or experiences many black Americans may have encountered. I think this becomes the product of immigrant parents and a childhood spent in a predominantly white space. I offered this potential solution to my friend, whose family could conduct the right genealogical searches and find enslaved plantation ancestors in Virginia and other southern states, whittling out existences on the hemline of river bends. My friend knew how to weave neat cornrows down someone's scalp and breathed in the steady beats of the gospel songs permeating the black church. Perhaps not having lived these details might have pushed me further to the edge of blackness.

"All of the above?" I asked my friend. "Something I haven't thought of too?"

"I still don't remember the comment, but I think 1, 2, and 4," she said, even as she apologized for the long-ago statement.

"Not to worry," I replied. My friend had many times over our long history done me the remarkable favor of forgiving and trying to understand my own worrisome statements that I had long forgotten. I could only do the same in return.

~

In January 1967, my father left Jamaica and arrived in New York City a month before he turned seventeen. His mother had gone before and prepared a trail for him to follow. He traveled with his younger sister and a knit hat that covered his ears. The warm Jamaican winds disappeared in his memory and made space for the frigid New York City winter. At his new school, Evander Childs High School in the Bronx, the building bulged with all types of students. White. Black. Brown. Those with firm, solid ties to this America and fresh arrivals like my father. My father says the groups stuck to themselves for the most part.

I imagine my father emerging from his basement apartment each day as wind whined in his ears and chilled his thin frame. He trudged down sidewalks gray as the winter day, then up the stairs on one side of the building to his first class. Sitting with a straight back, he listened to the clip and rush of accents, all new. When the bell rang and the students poured from the classrooms lining the hall, he crushed a notebook beneath his arm and looked away from the other students similar in appearance to him. Already he knew there was something about these black Americans that he wasn't.

Sneakers scuffed and squeaked against the tiled floor, and a couple in front of my father clasped hands. Someone pounded his fist against a metal locker and forced it to spring open. The shriek of the warning bell sent students swirling through this organized chaos.

Years later I asked my father about coming to America and about his high school. I asked about the other black students. "Did you fit in?"

My father looked at me, and he said something like, "I looked like them, but I didn't know what it was to be them."

~

The borders of blackness paint an image of a historical state of flux.

The words change across time, an attempt to capture perhaps a concept that cannot find containment.

Colored once upon a time. A grandmother figure used to watch me when I was a child. She wore her grayish-white hair pulled back away from the light brown of her face. She took unshelled nuts and used them as the heads for tiny dolls she made to amuse me during the long afternoons. Sometimes she watched her daily soaps while she brushed and braided my hair. She would say, "Don't look. Turn your head," so I couldn't catch a glimpse of adults living their sordid lives. And my grandma-like sitter used the word *colored* to refer to a black person, a term long out of vogue and, I now realize, situated her childhood deep in the past.

By then the use of the word *colored* had all but vanished. And the ensuing years of discord around terms such as *Negro* and *Afro-American* had dissipated into the country's general embrace of the word *black* to describe my babysitter, my family, and me. We were still a few years from the late eighties', early nineties' adoption of *African American.*[1] Cultural experts and politicians would argue for the term, saying that we also come from somewhere, just like German Americans and Chinese Americans.

My mother would later dismiss the term *African American* as too narrow for her, her sentiments matching words I would read about years later that spoke of the ways, "Americans have generally paid a great deal of attention to ethnic differences within the white race, while treating black Americans as if they were both a racial and an ethnic group with no intraracial differences."[2]

On a Sunday afternoon in our kitchen bubbling with the smells of a traditional Jamaican dinner, my mother spoke with a white friend. "I don't really like the term *African American,*" she explained. "I'm originally from Jamaica. I like *black.*" My mother didn't feel a connection to the implication of African geography in the words *African*

American. She saw herself excluded by the term, and she chose to embrace the word that encompassed her.

While our friend sat in one of our worn kitchen table chairs and I fluttered about nearby, pulling silverware from drawers and placing plates on the table, my mother stirred pots on the stove. Somewhere in this same conversation, our friend commented about black people looking so much alike. "No, no," my mother replied, and she pointed out different skin tones, different types of hair, great variations within a group of people.

During the 1970 United States Census, the government classi-fied people whose heritage stretched back to India as white.[3] When I learned this, I began to consider the permeable nature of the categories my country created. In a previous census this group had been called Hindu,[4] and in the 1980 census they became Asian Indian,[5] where they remain. The same year the US Census would have considered me to be half white, the 1970 questionnaire listed "Negro or Black."[6] By 2000 "African American" had been added to this category.[7]

My freshman year of college, my friend Zalenda—the child of Haitian immigrants—used to talk about the 1803 Haitian revolution while we all spoke about other people's campus crushes in her dorm room or moved to the hallway for a game of Spades. "Anyone who wasn't all black would have died," she said when she spoke about the uprising of the enslaved Africans—a revolt that brought freedom to the Caribbean nation and caused great fear to spread through the white masses in neighboring countries. It was a reversal of the typical one-drop rule, where one drop of black blood made a person black. In this case one drop of nonblack blood made a person not quite black enough to have made it through the revolution.

My friend shuffled the cards, dealt the deck, and pointed a finger at those who might have survived. I never would have made it. Neither would have others in our group.

"Oh, shut up, Zalenda," Jaime said, mock annoyance hiding the laughter about to break through. While we might not have had words to describe this reality, we all knew that what had separated us once hundreds of years ago no longer separated us now. I never minded my classification with the dead because I was never alone.

Just before winter break during my freshman year, the nonblack girls on my dorm floor talked about me and the other black girls. I heard the story later, much later, because I'd already left Pittsburgh and returned to Alaska for Christmas and colorful cookies, fresh pine-needle scent, and a rest from engineering problem sets and dormitory-style bathrooms. But my new friends—the friends who looked like me, the ones able to provide me with tips for my hair and baptism into their certain form of black culture—told me about it later.

While I was back in Anchorage, hunkered down in my childhood home, I received their e-mail. The nonblack girls had crowded into a dorm room on the night after the last final exams, our campus quiet with the impending emptying. With exams behind and the break ahead, people had time again to chat and laugh. And behind the partially closed door, those nonblack girls talked about my friends and talked about me.

Nina was walking down the hallway and heard everything. The way they said my name, the way they said that I was all right, that I was nice enough. But the other black girls. Well. That was a different story.

Nina with her black bob pushed the cracked door open. "Maybe next time you want to talk about other people, you should close your door." I envisioned her then turning one hundred and eighty degrees and walking out the door, leaving open mouths behind.

I read the e-mail at the computer in the basement of my Anchorage home while snow piled up in the yard. *So I'm "okay,"* I thought as the casual statement dragged me further from the circle my friends formed. *I don't want to be their "okay."*

~

The mid-1960s saw the beginnings of a major wave of twentieth-century Jamaican migration to the United States. The 1960 US Census counted almost 25,000 people originally from Jamaica.[8] But new legislation in 1965 relaxed the rigid quota system that had been in place since the 1920s, a system that favored Northern Europeans.[9] By 1970 the number of Jamaicans in the United States had almost tripled, to nearly 70,000.[10]

These Jamaican immigrants sold belongings, packed suitcases, and left their homes, filled with dreams and malleable hope for their new lives in America. And many of them—including my father's mother—moved to New York City. They carried their suitcases and found basement apartments offered by friends. They bought fuzzy hats and boots lined with faux fur and looked for jobs so they could begin to accumulate dollars. They thought of their families and the children they'd left behind.

When I ask my grandmother about her early days in New York, she often mentions a tour company based in her new city. "I took Casa Tours everywhere," she'll tell me. "And I was the only black." She states this fact with a level of pride, perhaps pride that she had touched the echelons of "white" activities in her newly immigrated life because this indicated success and a stable transition. My modern thinking shuffles in, and I want to add the word "person" to the end of her sentence. I want to explain to her that she is not a black, but rather she is a black person; the labels have shifted and changed across generations. She speaks about herself in a manner similar to the way my babysitter years ago called herself *colored*. But my grandmother has no less recognition than me that her brown skin sets her in a particular category in this country.

When I think of my grandmother saving her hard-earned dollars to take a trip with Casa Tours, I imagine her seated in a prim fashion, adorned with a wide-brimmed hat and dressed in a pleated skirt, on a bus full of white people. The only black person. But she wanted to take that tour, to see sights new and fresh, and she chose to enter and explore that world. Maybe she reveled in her ability to decide where she wanted to go and then choose that path.

Unlike my grandmother, when I travel to other cities, I rarely book tours. I take long walks through city blocks and use my phone and general good sense of direction to discover the places I want to find. One mild winter day I spent time in my nation's capital with plans to visit the African American museum near the national mall. In the final moments before the museum closed for the day, I stood staring at a map and a bar chart. "Five percent of black Americans are Afro-Caribbean," the words on the chart declared, information that caught me and my family up in the greatness of the structure where I stood. I found myself that day within the walls of the formidable building, several floors descending below the ground, several floors extending above. But I had arrived with time to see only one exhibit, to peruse the contents of one floor. I happened to choose the floor that would tell me how those like me—and my parents before and some of my grandparents too—have added to the nuance and wide definition of what it means to be a black American in my country.

Standing in that museum, I remembered how some people believe the word *black* should be capitalized when used to describe a person in America. Not *black*, but *Black*, capitalized as one might capitalize Irish or South African. I read of modern thinkers who tell me that black is not just a race, but it's also an ethnicity and so deserves a capital letter. Within the boundaries of the word resides people with shared cultural traditions and experiences beyond the color of their skin.

I find that when I look back over my writing over the passage of time, I never capitalize the word *black*, a label that I carry with a deep affiliation. I do believe that in this country being black *is* to embrace both a race and an ethnicity, so I wonder if I meet the qualifications for being *Black*. Do I fit the standards that allow me full acceptance in that group?

In my history I can fall back in time to my parents' Jamaican home and find ancestors once held in slavery, forced to build the very house my grandmother grew up in. Once my friend's comment about not thinking of me as black pointed out the reality of a person being both a particular race and *also* something more. Does my experience align well enough to live with a capitalized *B*?

By choosing to use the lowercase *b*, I am saying that I want to be included in this definition. I want the word to be expansive enough to draw me within the curves and twists of the letters.

The day I stared at that bar chart listing migration patterns of Afro-Caribbeans to the United States, I really wasn't supposed to have accessed the museum. An hour before the museum closed for the day, I had arrived in the shadow of the front entrance. The structure of the walls flared out above where I stood, leaving me standing in a sunless spot. Behind me the afternoon sun cast rays of late daylight on the lawn that edged the museum and jutted out to the road. Three black women sat on a low concrete wall separating the walkway from the muted grass. They rested in casual poses, the weight of standing taken from their legs, evidence of a long day of ushering crowds of people through the museum's doors.

"Do you have a ticket?" one of the women called to me.

I knew the museum required tickets, advance ones secured

months ago or same-day ones secured in the early hours of morning. But I also knew of the afternoon tickets, available just past lunchtime. At this time of day, the museum must be on a path toward empty, I had reasoned. There must be room for one more.

"All the tickets are gone for the day," one of the other women told me. The three of them were older, not my mother's age but ten maybe fifteen years older than me. They'd seen much of life in this country that I hadn't. I was sure of this. One of the women looked at me. Her eyes took me in with a single glance, from my head to my feet. I wondered if she thought what I thought: that I need to see this museum, that it was important for a woman like me to see inside the walls.

"You're just getting off work?" she asked in a comforting way that was less a question and more of a statement of knowing me. I explained that I was here for a conference, visiting from out of town. I watched the three look up to where I stood. Their expressions changed to a sweet pity, and they motioned me toward the entrance. They pointed me through the revolving doors into a place where I think they knew that somewhere I would see myself.

On that mild day in my nation's capital, I was part of the circle of women resting on a low wall, the ones who motioned me forward. *I am with them and like them*, I thought as I pushed against the revolving door, crossed the museum threshold, and walked in.

Chapter 14

Recalling What Was Good

A new friend talks with me about Alaska. "I've only met one other person from there," she says. I smile as I think that she's met one more person than most people who begin this conversation with me.

"What's it like?" she asks.

I pause before I speak, just as I do with so many others when I answer this question because there isn't enough time to flesh out the reality of the beauty and tension, the piercing cold winters and the long-awaited spring. A quick reply can't contain the nuance of a childhood I hold close in the form of photographs of what my family once was and the memories of the life we shared together. All of us. My mother and father, my sister and me.

I look at this new friend, and I think there will be more conversations to come, more moments when additional stories about my life in the forty-ninth state will surface, providing a fuller picture than I can create in this response. So for now I tell her about the wonder of Alaska. I speak of the mountains and inlets, the length of the summer sun. And whether I say this or not, I find myself recalling all that was good.

Riverbank Trivia

Sometimes on one of those languid summer evenings during my Alaskan childhood, the hope for fresh salmon sent my parents into a swirl of motion. My father rummaged through the garage and gathered his fishing pole, net, and tackle box. My mother spread margarine over slices of soft white bread before she piled them high with thin-sliced ham and slid the completed sandwiches into Ziploc bags. Then, with the evening still an Alaskan summer bright, my sister, my parents, and I scooted into our seats in the blue Subaru and journeyed several hours south to the Russian River.

There my father yanked on hip waders and joined a gaggle of other fishermen hoping to catch their daily allowance of salmon: two fish that night and two more after the clock moved into a new day. My sister, my mother, and I skipped the cold evening air, roaring water, and stench of dead salmon down by the riverbank. We chose to remain in the car and eat sandwiches and play a Bible trivia game, glancing at the shadows creeping close, waiting for my father to return.

A few years ago, while sorting through old stuff at my mother's house, I found the familiar trivia game. I stood in the garage filled with books and boxes, old shoes and dust. Stood there holding the weight of the game, surrounded by the raw images of nostalgia. There in the packed room, I returned to the back of a long-gone Subaru and the time when my parents shared a house and a life.

I saw my little-girl body on the passenger side, my sister across the space between, my mother turned in her seat. Beyond the car windows, a timid dark swallowed the long Alaskan day. My sister, my mother, and I splayed trivia cards and quizzed each other for hours.

"Name four of Jesus' disciples."

"Who was Samuel's mother?"

"What did God create on the second day?"

We waited until well past midnight, when my father returned to the driver's seat, his shirt sleeves damp from the currents, his being saturated with the strong smell of outside and fresh-caught salmon. With the dawn soon ready to overcome the dim of night, my father steered our car home. The soft roll of my parents' voices lulled their daughters into a thick sleep.

Funeral Song

"Sing this at my funeral," my father says. My father, my sister, and I sit in a row across the grayish-blue upholstered seats in the front of my father's Chevy truck—the one vehicle I remember from childhood that my parents purchased brand new. My father sits behind the steering wheel, his seat pushed back much further than the passenger side my sister and I share. The extra space accommodates his tall body.

I sit in the middle, where I can reach out and press the buttons on the radio and skip tracks on the Kingston Trio cassette whirling through the tape player. We have our favorites: "Lemon Tree," "Where Have All the Flowers Gone," and the one about the man who never returned, stuck forever on the Boston subway with never enough money to pay his exit fee. My sister sits to my right, where she can lean her head against the window when she chooses. On a day like many Saturdays before and many more Saturdays after, days when my sister and I rotate positions in the truck, we switch between cassette tapes and Paul Harvey's calm radio voice telling us the rest of the story. Sometimes my father turns off the radio, sucking the sound from the car. He then says we should practice his funeral song.

"Listen to me sing this," he says. "I want you to sing it at my funeral." We head through the slow roads of Anchorage, around the nearly perpendicular bend on DeArmoun Road, over the railroad tracks, but where we head, I can't say. Mountains hang behind us, great peaks almost always capped with snow. The inlet extends nearby—around a corner, across an expanse of trees, out there in some unseen distance.

My father begins the song, "Oh! My Pa-Pa."[1] His voice is low and drenched in melancholy, bursting with exaggerated dramatics, singing words about a wonderful father who is now gone. He lifts his right arm from the wheel, his index finger transformed to a conductor's baton. He nods in our direction and motions for us to join.

And join we do, high-pitched off-key treble voices of little girls woven together with our father's bass. My sister and I sing about the day my father will leave us as fatherless daughters. A day so far in the future, a day really so impossible that all we can do is laugh and sing and raise our arms in front of us as if together we conduct the greatest symphony anyone could imagine.

Robot Dreams

Back when we lived in the beige split-level house at the base of the Anchorage hillside, my father bought a robot. During the day, while my parents were at work and the babysitter watched her soaps, I crept down both sets of stairs. I stopped on the final step and flattened my body against the textured wall. My torso and legs remained motionless, but I stretched my neck around the corner. There in the empty basement stood a shiny metal cylinder much like R2-D2. Perhaps, I thought, if I watched long enough, I might see it sail across the brown carpet as it had done when my father hovered near the machine.

Years later, long after we left that house and my parents had left their marriage, I asked my mother about the robot. "Your father was trying to start a business. People could hire the robot for events." She searched her memory to recall details. "Perhaps to help market things, advertise at malls or something." She told me the business never gained much traction beyond being a cute novelty. Eventually my father placed a "for sale" ad in our local Anchorage newspaper. Someone just outside of Glenallen, almost two hundred miles away, came to buy my father's costly investment on a payment plan. "I don't think we ever recovered more than the initial down payment," my mother recalled.

I heard the story and remembered the shiny metal, the way the silver cylinder remained motionless most days. I grasped a hazy picture of the one or two times when I saw my father hold a rectangular object and make the robot glide toward me, move through the void space that separated us.

With my mother's words, I saw my father as less of a character in the story of a broken marriage and more of a human being with broken dreams.

Fish Camp

The summer I am eight, I climb narrow stairs and board a five-seater airplane. My sister sits next to me, my mother ahead. Beyond the city limits of Anchorage, across the gray water of Cook Inlet, in Beluga, my father waits to fold arms around his daughters. As his family's arrival approaches, I imagine, he thinks of his lips pressed against his wife's and his arm resting on her shoulder. He walks with a light foot, and a thin whistle announces his presence to branches and rocks and birds from the sea. Through a worn path in the woods, he emerges by the edge of the makeshift runway—a strip of land cleared of trees.

This summer, like the summer before and maybe the summer

after, my father has left his family behind in Anchorage. He has traded in his school-year suits and alphabet ties for a summer job complete with rubber hip waders and a commercial fisherman's boat. But for a week this year and last year and next year, too, my mother, sister, and I join him in his one-room cabin on the beach.

The cabin stands on stilts and lets the ashen waves of high tide rush beneath the floor of our temporary home. In this place salty sea wind flutters past our noses, tinted with the scent of salmon. My sister and I inhale and exhale the air and the wind and the freedom of the beach. A backdrop of cabins rises behind us while we build sandcastles and let the foamy water chase us across the sand. In those moments, our child eyes move past the waves and settle on the string of boats touching our horizon. Out there, at the edge of what we see, my father casts his net upon the water and hopes large salmon might lodge themselves in the mesh grid.

My sister and I, we fill our days with hunts for treasure—shells, bright stones, or a smoothed piece of broken glass. Far out in the inlet current, my father grabs at the fibers of the net and pulls trapped fish from between the gaps, salmon slime covering his arms. Sometimes I imagine my father beyond my line of sight, past the confines of the inlet, out on the real sea. So close to where the mighty water decides one's course and determines one's destiny.

Those summers in Beluga vanish. Family vacations and camps for growing girls transform commercial fishing summers into a burden. Rather than exchanging suits for hip waders, my father pulls on jeans and T-shirts. By the time I reach ten or eleven, Beluga, the beach, the string of boats at the edge of my known world become the stuff of stories. The crescent mouth that recalls a sweet past. A moment remembered when a waitress tells me of the salmon special. A moment forgotten until I watch the great waves of high tide on an overcast day.

114

Now I know seas and oceans and the horizons of distant lands. I am familiar with the metallic gleam of O'Hare, and I can speak of the wide corridors of Heathrow. Sliding my passport across the counter in Cape Town or Kuala Lumpur feels natural, like a skill mastered long ago. But sometimes my face stares through the miniature window of a jumbo jet at the glint of water reflecting a bright sun. In a rare moment when the ocean below appears that perfect blend of blue and gray, my nose instantly remembers salt air together with the sour smell of salmon. I am then inside a five-seater flying machine growling with the engine's roar, twirling higher in the sky. Across an inlet, my father steps along a sandy beach and walks up a narrow path. He emerges beside a dirt runway that returns to him a wife and two small girls.

Lemonade Stand

Two circles of particle board and a thick cylinder of wood. You built a table tall enough for Laurel and me to stand behind and pour juice or lemonade into paper cups. I collected the money. Laurel poured the juice. Mom brought more drinks in plastic Tupperware pitchers. And you, you were away at work, getting your school ready for another year, but of course you were present each time our fingers touched the table's flat surface or rubbed the rough edges. You were there when our final customer pressed coins into my hand, a small boy's thirst quenched by the tangy drink and the sappy smiles offered by little girls. And you were there when Laurel and I helped Mom roll the table back into the garage through the center of your empty parking space.

Mom, Laurel, and I ate dinner on the deck that evening. Was it that evening or maybe another so much like it? But never mind—we ate dinner that evening on the porch as the summer sun streaked yellow and gold across the blue sky. Even though you needed to work late, I saw you in that fourth chair next to me, unoccupied. Later I heard your voice in the book Mom read to us that night while Laurel and I sucked on homemade juice popsicles. And even later still, I knew your footsteps would creak against the carpeted floor after Mom flicked out our bedroom lights for the night. I would dream well under the comfort of a warm blanket—dream of telling you stories about our lemonade stand and of counting pennies, nickels, and dimes with you the next day.

Chapter 15

Plucked and Planted

One day, after I had moved to Charlotte, my sister, who lived several hours away in Chapel Hill, called me as she drove toward my home. "Vegetable oil," she asked, "do you have any?"

I rummaged through the bottles of olive oil and sesame oil, balsamic vinegar and red wine vinegar too. "I don't think so," I said, the phone pressed firm into my ear. "No," I confirmed a moment later, my interest now piqued. My next question wanted to know her reason for asking. "Plantains," she told me. "I just bought plantains, and I want to fry them." She said plantains must be fried in vegetable oil. Her quick, matter-of-fact voice placed the emphasis on *must*.

My sister knows things that I don't. One afternoon we walked into a grocery store, and she spotted a display of mangoes. She selected a large fruit with green and red mottled skin from the display and lifted the manifestation of our childhood to her nose. She sniffed the mango, the length of her dark hair pulled back, circling the crown of her head, framing her face. I imagined that somewhere in the recesses of her mind, she hurtled for a moment in the direction of Jamaica.

She held the fruit another minute before she returned it to the

117

mound of its siblings and reached for another and then another. The wide hem of her trademark broomstick skirt swayed along with her movements. After each inhale of the musk of a mango, she declared the fruit in question not ripe, not likely to be very good, not something we should place gingerly in our basket and watch the cashier weigh as we bought our groceries.

Not long ago I asked my sister if she remembered our father eating mangoes for his after-dinner snack. Did she recall how he'd kneel next to our parents' bed while our mother sipped a mug of warm milk nearby? "How did he eat the fruit?" I asked. "In separate pieces? How did he tackle the pit?" All I could recall was our father hunched over an old blue towel spread across a chunk of the bed, a white plate edged with navy-blue flowers, and the juice splattering across his fingers and dribbling near his mouth.

Without even a moment to think about the old memory, my sister said, "He'd slice it, then pull the flesh off the skin with his teeth. At the end he'd just suck the fruit off the pit." When she told me these facts, I remembered them afresh.

I often think about how my sister and I are not like our parents. We ate the curried chicken our mother prepared with the cubes of potatoes stained yellow with gravy. We split fried dumplings in half and spread butter over their doughy centers. We pinched strips of fried plantains cooling on a plate next to the stove. But my sister and I, we speak with the blocky tones of American accents.

When our parents used to make us repeat Jamaican patwa phrases, they corrected our usage and pronunciation. Sometimes I tried hard to wrap my mouth around the words and shape my tongue in the right way. "Not 'Wah going on?'" our mother might say, "but 'Wah gwaan?'" She'd repeat as she opened her mouth and stretched the final vowels long enough that we could peek down her throat. More often I found it easier not to play along.

My sister, though, she would ask our parents to repeat the phrase once and then again. She'd shape her tongue to make the syllables and practice the cadence in such a way that showed how much she cared. None of us were surprised when she chose Jamaica for her sixth-grade country report. When my turn came, I picked a European country, like the rest of my classmates did. I never considered choosing my parents' homeland.

I think a thread reached from the depths of the Caribbean, crossed water and land, and wrapped itself around two sisters' souls. Somehow that thread pulled my sister closer. Something shrank the distance in her mind, and many years later—long after we'd both left Alaska—she would speak to the woman behind the counter at a Jamaican grocery store. "Coco bread, beef patties," she'd request, choosing to copy the familiar lilt and knowing of people who share a common heritage.

"You must fry plantains in vegetable oil," she told me. "You *must*."

During my childhood in Alaska, plantains came from the Carrs Quality Center on Gambell Street near downtown Anchorage, clear across town from our regular grocery store. Our normal Carrs boasted proximity to our house, a shiny, modern layout, and bunches of yellow bananas stacked one atop the other. But no plantains. So every now and then, our mother would push my sister and me in a cart through narrow aisles in the outdated Gambell store. On lucky days she found a display of green plantains near a mound of common bananas.

For the next week or so, the plantains sat in the wire fruit basket hanging from our kitchen ceiling. Days passed, and the ripening yellow seeped into the green peels. Black streaks and splotches appeared with a sort of brazen resolve to conquer. Then on the right day—a day I think my sister would just know—my mother peeled the fruit, sliced the pale orange flesh into strips, and took a plastic spatula to turn the sweet plantains blistering in a puddle of oil.

I sat on the crimson stool pushed near the counter, and my sister hovered close by. We waited for my mother to lift the plantains from the pan and set them on a plate lined with a paper towel. After a moment she offered us the first taste. My fingers warmed with the hot food. We took. We consumed, savoring the comfort of the caramelized edge. We took more.

The first time I fried a plantain, I was a newlywed and living in South Africa, where I'd met my husband. A friend from Cameroon slid a half-ripe plantain across the width of my kitchen counter. "I have a friend with a tree," she said. Often she and I would talk about foods we both knew, foods hard to find at the local Pick n Pay.

I think now of the way I express deep Jamaican affinities in my public interactions that I don't always live in my private life. In moments when my cultural lineage becomes a connection point in a shared conversation, I commiserate with another. I use words like *longing* and *craving* for foods I know I'm content to eat without regularity.

I hugged my friend that day and waited for the mustard yellow to consume the remaining green peel and for the black marks of ripeness to appear. One day I took my thumb and index finger and pressed against the ripe fruit. The flesh caved in a bit, and I could hear my mother or sister telling me the plantain was ready.

I grabbed a cutting board and a sharp knife and prepared a pan with a small pool of hot oil. I ate each amber-colored strip while standing near the stove. Greasy fingers brought more and more of the familiar taste to my mouth until nothing remained but the oil-soaked paper towel. I tossed the peel into the garbage and washed the pan. The smell of sweet, starchy fruit browning in popping oil lingered throughout the kitchen and the rest of my home.

On a New Year's Day, years after my sister and I had established our adult lives, we dipped French fries in ketchup and ate hamburgers in a restaurant with orange walls and laminate tabletops—a place that felt so American. My sister asked if I'd read a particular essay about our country's first black president—a man with a white mother from Kansas and a black father from Kenya. She spoke of our president's assertion that he chose to enmesh himself in black American culture.[1]

I think we both thought of our black Jamaican parents and the way they arrived in this country so unfamiliar with being black Americans. At once we nodded our heads at each other, two sisters mirroring the other, a mutual act of recognition at an idea resonating with both.

"You made a choice. You chose being black," my sister said to me, her words not about the color of my skin but about where I'd found a sense of connectivity.

I replied with the word *opportunity* and reminded my sister that I'd left the remote isolation of Alaska and ventured across the country to college. I mentioned the black girls on my dorm floor and the way they had extended offers of friendship. My father once told me that I became a black American in college. I think what he meant was while at Carnegie Mellon, my friends had led me to a cultural identity beyond just a box to select my race. Like President Obama, I found *black* to be a place to belong.

My sister heard my explanation. "You made a choice," she repeated. "I think I missed my chance. I think I missed out." The mellow smell of white potatoes fried in oil—vegetable, perhaps?—settled through the space.

Long ago, when my sister and I were small girls and our mother pushed us in a shopping cart through the grocery store, strangers would stop her, admire her daughters, and ask if we were twins.

"Separated by twenty months," I say now whenever I recount the story of those two brown-skinned sisters.

I go back two generations and see our black grandmothers, our Indian grandfathers, and even further back, a white great-great from England. Together these shades of skin, different countries and cultures, formed future generations beneath a vast umbrella of being Jamaican. So my sister looks like me and yet not. My sister thinks like me and yet not. In this country our paths diverged. Now I peddle speculation and theories as to the reasons.

Around the same time that strangers used to ask if my sister and I were twins, our parents left us one evening in the care of our babysitter. At snack time we both climbed on stools pushed near the counter. Our babysitter peeled back the skin of a banana. She sliced the fruit through the center and placed each half on a separate plate. "Too hard," we said as we pushed our plates away. The babysitter tucked the two halves back in the open peel and crimped the skin shut as well as she could, as if this action might in the future hatch a ripe fruit.

Later that evening when our parents returned home, my mother said, "My good, good plantain," when she looked at the plantain mistaken for a banana and peeled much too early. I like to think my sister reached out and touched my mother's arm. Whether this is true or not, I imagine that somewhere inside, my sister knew the difference too.

A plantain is not a banana, but they are close. They both share common ancestry with the same ancient plant. The seeds of modern varieties are sterile. Instead of sowing seeds to yield new fruit, immature suckers are taken from the parent and planted elsewhere.[2]

Just after I finished graduate school, my mother took me to visit Jamaica. During that trip, I told my uncle in Kingston that I was Jamaican. He shook his head no. I laughed, but I think this gesture directed to my sister would have hurt her. When my friend with a similar complexion to mine told me that she didn't really think of me as being black, a great sadness gripped me. I think a lesser sadness would have gripped my sister. Perhaps we are both whole and yet both incomplete. If my sister missed out, I missed out too.

I've heard people say that one day my sister and I will be all we have left to know the extent of our whole lives. The time will come when we have neither a living mother or father, but she will have me, and I will have her—two people who have known each other across the vastness of our existence.

Then, I think, I will pull up a chair in her kitchen and watch her knead together flour, water, and baking powder for the golden-fried dumplings. She'll sauté onions in a pan, bits of tomato too. She'll drain the ackee, so yellow in color I'll think of the tropical sun. I'll breathe the aroma that transports us together back to our mother's kitchen. And I'll feel a hard rush of gratitude at the way her path compressed the distance between Anchorage and Kingston and between our childhood and our parents' beginnings.

Many years ago I told my sister, "I don't need a second mother"— as if her twenty additional months could ever really give her that role. But on that day so far in the future, when we will have only each other, the only two who have lived all the memories, I believe she'll show me how to sniff a mango for ripeness, what a plantain looks like when it's ready to fry, and how much coconut milk to add to the rice and peas.

Then I'll think, and perhaps I'll say, "You didn't miss out." I didn't miss out either. We are each plucked and planted our own particular distance from a far-off island adrift in the sea.

Chapter 16

A Lingering Thread

One spring I met my friend Shalini for coffee. We sat outside beneath a wide umbrella that cast a pleasant shadow over our seats. "A black woman and an Indian woman," onlookers would have said of us had they given thought to our ethnicities. Me with my deep brown skin and pile of tight black curls. Shalini with her lighter brown skin and slick, dark hair.

That afternoon Shalini told me about the thriving Indian community in Charlotte. I smiled when she shared. I thought of her gathered with friends, acquaintances, perhaps even strangers in neighborhood clubhouses or the banquet room at the back of a restaurant. People clothed in shiny fabric and bright colors, swirling around the length and width of the festive space. Tables holding rich curries and baskets piled high with naan, roti, and other breads. Vibrant music thumping through the air, familiar notes sweeping people into movement. Men in loose clothing tapping the rhythm with their feet. Young woman spinning across the wooden tiles of the dance floor. I imagined Shalini's head tossed back, laughing.

But what I didn't see was myself as part of that group. I couldn't create an image of me sitting comfortably at a table there, laughing with friends and acquaintances. I couldn't see myself dressed in richly colored cloth that shimmered beneath dimmed lights.

Years ago, during my freshman year of college, I had decided to join Mayur—the student organization that promoted heritage and culture for those connected to India. I knew that most people thought I looked like a black woman, and I knew all of my grandparents had been born and raised in Jamaica. However, when I thought of my mother's Indian father and my father's Indian father, I wondered if half of me might fit with these students. My Indian ancestors had arrived in Jamaica generations ago as laborers and indentured servants, but still they were Indian. And because of two Indian grandfathers, I thought perhaps I belonged with Mayur just as much as I belonged with the group for black students.

Except during the first meeting I saw I didn't belong with Mayur. That evening I hovered near the wall and watched the other students share something I couldn't access. They spoke with great fluctuations in tone about music and movies, food and more. From time to time, a few shifted into a language I had never heard. Even though they smiled and said, "Hi Patrice. We're glad you're here," I still disappeared after the meeting ended. Laughter and conversation faded from my ears as I exited the building and walked toward my dorm room in a curtain of twilight dropping over a mild autumn night.

London, United Kingdom

Raised in India, my friend Shamik knows things I want to know, so I ask him questions at the little Indian restaurant down the road from the Bayswater tube station during my junior year abroad. Our other friends surround us, and we spoon vivid curries from shallow, brass-colored

*bowls. Here I order naan, large pieces of warm flat bread with a random
sprinkling of coin-sized black circles. They taste and feel close to the rotis
I grew up eating. The aromas of cumin and coriander and other smells I
can't name hover across the restaurant.*

*In between bites of food, I tell Shamik about my ties to India. I men-
tion my mother's father's family. Even more I talk of my father's father's
family. "The British gave my father's family a new name when they arrived
in Jamaica. My father changed it to Harduar as an adult—after the town
he had heard his family came from—but we have a u and not a w." My
voice quiets.*

*"Doorway to the gods," Shamik tells me. "That's what the place your
last name comes from means." Shamik tells me this city is a holy place, an
area where people travel to bathe in the River Ganges. In this moment of
information, I now know more about my last name than my father ever
did. He knew the word, but somewhere over great space and decades of
time, the meaning became lost.*

*Doorway to the gods. I turn the phrase around in my mind, let it sit
there and think of a faraway city where people pilgrimage.*

*Shamik has handed me something. A gift of knowing? An offering of
a link? The talk of the table shifts to other subjects. My lips move, and my
voice laughs at the right moments. My eyes follow the flow of conversation
and indicate that I'm listening. But I'm not present. My mind wanders,
and I think about translation and meaning and doorway to the gods.*

My father grew up with the last name *Williams*, the same last
name the British officials gave his grandfather when he arrived in
Jamaica, becoming part of the British Empire's decades-old plan to
supply labor to their colonies. Eleven years after the British abolished
slavery, a ship of Indian laborers disembarked in Jamaica. The year
was 1845. Two hundred sixty-one people arrived that first year. When
the practice of indenture ended in 1921, approximately thirty-six

thousand Indians had—over the many decades—arrived in Jamaica.[1] The cessation of the free labor my African ancestors once provided to Jamaica made space for the cheap labor my Indian ancestors brought to that place.

Over the years my father shared of whispers and stories and mentions in his childhood of a place called Harduar back in his grandparents' first home. "That's who they were before," my father said. And I would imagine him as a child, a slight boy shuffling around adult conversation and hearing snippets about a mysterious place whose name, I would later learn, was actually called Hardwar.

In my Internet searches, I have seen black-and-white pictures of Indian indentured servants posed in front of a great rock formation in Jamaica. Vines and trees block the sky and let a mere dribble of sunlight into the frame. The men mostly stand at the back; the women and children sit or crouch at the front. Yards of fabric cover their bodies and wrap around their heads.

Their stoic faces share nothing of what they might think, so I conjure guesses about them. I imagine the families they formed in this new place and try to envision the families they left behind. I think of the older girls hunched over great cast-iron pots, stirring the evening meal while the young children haul water from a nearby stream. And in this way, I come up with ideas about my own relatives too.

Were my great-grandparents dreamers like me? Did they arrive in Jamaica thinking they would amass wealth and one day return home? By the time my grandfather was born, were their palms and feet callused from years of labor? Were their bodies thin and worn from plantation life, from illness that spread across humid air through the wind? These are things my father doesn't know, things I can only assume.

When my father became a US citizen, America offered him the chance to change his name. Somewhere in a cramped office choking with paperwork and applications, he filled capital letters into boxes on a form. He hesitated a moment before guessing at the spelling of a word he had heard but never before seen in print. And so he became a Harduar. When I was born years later, I would be a Harduar too.

My father has been known to say, "Maybe a *w* would have been a better choice."

Once I watched a TED talk in which writer Pico Iyer, who is of Indian ancestry, spoke about the movement of people. A few minutes into his talk, he said, "One hundred percent of my blood and ancestry does come from India. Except, I've never lived one day of my life there. I can't speak even one word of its more than twenty-two thousand dialects. So I don't think I've really earned the right to call myself an Indian."[2]

"Earned the right to call myself Indian." I thought about this phrase, forgot about it, and inevitably returned to it later. Have I earned the right to call myself Indian? Or partially Indian? Half Indian? Fifty percent?

I wrote an essay once that mentioned my multiracial heritage. I was taking a writing class and wrote about my Indian grandfather on my father's side and my Indian grandfather on my mother's side. Half Indian, half black, I wrote and shared with my class. When I finished, I set my essay in front of me on the long table we clustered around. One person, then another, and another leaned toward me. "Don't you mean one quarter Indian?" Their kind eyes and quizzical mouths formed questions to help me catch my mistake. "You meant to write one quarter, didn't you?"

"No," I said. "One half. Two Indian grandfathers. Two black grandmothers. One half."

Later that evening, long after we gathered our pens, our papers, our notebooks and bags and exited into a quiet night dotted with starlight, I stared in the mirror at my brown skin. I looked for threads of Indian heritage running through the features of a black woman. Because that's what I call myself. That's where I proudly identify when asked to check a box.

A black woman.

A black American.

A black Jamaican American.

But also a black Jamaican American with Indian ancestry. A black Jamaican American who is part Indian. Half Indian. In blood and ancestry and perhaps little more.

Sub-Saharan Africa

We were plucked from the land, chained together, packed into the cargo holds of great ships. Many died on that journey across the Middle Passage. Those who endured faced a living death. And I arise from those survivors.

In the PBS series *African American Lives*, Henry Louis Gates Jr., a professor at Harvard, helped black Americans learn about their ancestry. In the final episode of the program, participants stood before mirrors, opened their mouths, and swabbed their cheeks. I watched as they waited for the results of highly specialized and specific genetic and DNA testing.

The results allowed Gates to direct some participants to specific regions of the African continent from which their ancestors came. For a few he could even provide the names of people groups connected to a participant's lineage. Gates took comedian Chris Tucker to Angola, where his particular ancestral people group lives today. A sort of welcome home for this long-lost relative.[3] But this was the extent of what Gates could offer—a fairly certain belief that Tucker descended from this group of people but perhaps not that particular village, not that particular place. Gates placed Tucker as close as possible without finding a certain dot on a map.

That day in Angola, the sun shone crisp and crinkly and golden. The sky expanded in sweet-as-honey blue. And I forgot for a moment the depravity of ships carrying human cargo and the way each generation that arises loses a bit more and bit more until little exists except the common story of how black people were taken from Africa and brought to the Americas.

In my family the generations removed since India are many. Perhaps not as many as the generations removed since the African continent. However, enough time has elapsed that the things that made my ancestors related to India by more than just blood have dissipated into broad phrases, such as Indo-Jamaican and Indo-Caribbean. The long-ago movement gave rise to a new type of person, a legacy from a far-off place with a culture rooted in a fusion of many.

But I claim India. Perhaps I claim it because I am a black woman in America. From the beginning I have lived under the weight of that common story of people ripped from far-off lands and enslaved in this country.

Long ago, in a class where I was the only black student, a social studies teacher asked for my comments—and only my comments—about a movie depicting slavery. What did I think? Was it okay? Was it accurate? He gave me a simple story with no way outside that narrative. Brown-skinned people like me all go back to Africa, the story goes. Black people all come from a gigantic, vague mass of land on the other side of the Middle Passage.

Maybe I claim India because being part Indian becomes about being part black. There are stories, unknown stories that roll across the salty waves of the open sea. Unknown stories contained in the hulls of rundown ships carrying enslaved human beings. And there are known stories of my Indian ancestors arriving on Jamaican shores. I am a story, and I cling to the known parts because maybe in that act I remember and also remind others how much has been taken, erased, and lost. I am here, and there is a story of me that connects back to a place in India called Hardwar in the Indian state of Uttarakhand. What also exists is another story of me that winds back across the Atlantic Ocean to an unknown place and an unknown dot on the vast continent of Africa.

I think I lift my voice in subtle protest when I mention India. I say to those who hear me that we with our brown skin are not all the same, that even those who trace all lines straight back through the Middle Passage, even those people are rooted in a particular spot, a precise place, even if unknown. They are not just part of a whole continent with one name that sucks in all, stirs them around, and produces a common thing.

My maiden name becomes a doorway for me to remember that stories happened—both the known and the unknown. Washed away in the tides of history is the intimacy with cultures that might help me know what it means to belong to those places. To a specific known in India. To a precise unknown on the African continent. But the effects of the past, known and unknown, linger even today.

Hardwar (or Haridwar), Uttarakhand, India

I travel to Hardwar. Not on a plane or via a boat as my ancestors would have traveled perhaps a century ago. Instead I open a webpage, navigate to Google Maps, and type in Hardwar. Google Maps takes me to an unfamiliar chunk of the world many meridians away. A red line delineates modern boundaries of the ancient city. When I click on satellite pictures, the shape of the city fills with the brown of rooftops, buildings, and roads. A lush green extends outside the border.

Where to look? I wonder. What am I trying to see? I pick an area at random, zoom in close enough to stare at hundreds of rooftops and roads snaking and curving through the city into angles and twists and shapes of the letter Y.

There my journey ends. I can zoom in no further. Did I find what I was looking to see? My heart wasn't stirred beyond a desire to visit a new place. I didn't feel a need to walk through ancestral streets or a hope to return to an ancient home.

I close the satellite image and return to the life I breathe.

Sometimes my father tells a story his father told him. Many years before my father's birth, my grandfather's uncle suggested he and my grandfather leave Jamaica and go to India. I think perhaps that uncle had been born in India and carried memories of the place across months of water.

Maybe that uncle remembered what it was like to walk down familiar roads where footsteps and the wheels of wooden carts kicked clouds of dust high in the air. Maybe aspects of Jamaica reminded him of that place across the globe. Something had tangled him into a life of labor, and he'd agreed to sign on to an indenture of service and sail to Jamaica. He arrived to murky conditions, and I imagine there were moments when the sun pierced passing storm clouds in just the right way and he remembered his childhood. When the breeze held a whiff that smelled of the earth in his home, he remembered. Something existed that called him back to that eastern land, a whisper he couldn't ignore.

These things, I think, prompted that uncle to book passage on a mighty ship destined to cross oceans and months later to arrive on India's shore. And I believe that uncle convinced my grandfather, a man like Pico Iyer who had never stepped foot in India, who perhaps didn't even know a word of any of the many dialects, to leave his Jamaican home and try a distant place.

"This is not your home. Not really your home," I imagine my grandfather's uncle saying to him while he tossed a few meager belongings into a thin bag.

I see my grandfather on an old-fashioned deck with large, white sails and a Union Jack flapping high above. He stares to the shore of the land that birthed him. Then he turns to the wide-open ocean, trying to see across the water beyond where it blends into a dull horizon. He stares again to the shore, again to the water. Then he turns to his uncle and explains that he can't leave this place. He wants to hold what is known because there exists so much unknown.

His uncle's pleading words—"Come with me!"— muddle his thoughts. But in the harbor aboard the ship, my father tells me, my grandfather changed his mind. He left his uncle standing on the ship's deck, jumped into the water, and swam back to the shore.

My grandfather—I think he knew something I only begin to understand. The ties that bind us are thin; the threads that connect fray. In every person there exists an element of the past that we want to grasp. *See me,* we say. *I am rooted in an identifiable place. I am descended from a particular people.* A yearning endures that perhaps cannot be satisfied by claiming ethnicities or strengthening connections with other lands. In the end, across oceans and continents, we move from east to west, north to south, country to country, place to place, and our family lines are irrevocably changed.

My grandfather said goodbye to his uncle and jumped into water so warm and so clear. His arms cut through the slight waves, and his body assumed an untethered existence. Far from his ancestral home, new life emerged. Experiences gave rise to new creation, and my grandfather's body became an arrow destined for a place he considered home.

Part III

So Then How Do We Live?

If I rise on the wings of the dawn,
    if I settle on the far side of the sea,
even there your hand will guide me,
    your right hand will hold me fast.

—Psalm 139:9–10

Chapter 17

Beyond What I Could Imagine

During my high school years, I spent many winter evenings tucked away in my bedroom, surrounded by my lavender walls, beneath my comforter, with a pen in hand. The Alaskan winter, with its cold and dark, pressed against my window, the panes icy to the touch, the shadows and dusk together a cloak around me—at once both a comfort and a state of severity.

In the hushed quiet of near night, I offered faint prayers to the blank pages of my spiral notebook. Just before I switched off my bedside lamp, I let my words and desires consume the page. College on the East Coast. Time spent living overseas. And one day the son of Jamaican immigrants for a husband—a guy with a history like mine. I wanted to add further precision to that request, to say that he should come from Alaska, too, but I thought that might have been beyond the realm of acceptable prayer boundaries. While I'd been taught to believe in God's infinite power, I considered that even God must have limits. If this man, this son of Jamaican immigrants, were from Alaska, surely my family—and I—would already know him. I wanted to marry someone of flesh and bones, not a mystical being.

SO THEN HOW DO WE LIVE?

Only someone like the son of Jamaican immigrants could under-stand what it means to live as me, I told myself, my wide cursive script reaching for the sweep of adolescent dreams. I thought of this idea as I walked the halls of my mostly white high school and studied brochures from distant universities. I stared at pictures of their thick lawns to determine whether they were the right shade of academic green. I looked for oak or maple trees I could imagine myself seated below in a circle of friends, the blades of grass prickly against my ankles and palms. I scanned the information for a chance to study overseas.

More than a decade later, in early June, I leave behind my Alaskan summer. I arrive in a Cape Town winter that holds the city in a shivering trance, replete with misty mornings, a handful of bright days, and an everlasting cold requiring the bulk of sweaters and scarves.

"What brings you to Cape Town?" the immigration officer asks. By now I've accumulated a variety of colorful stamps in the stiff pages of my passport, and I've sat beneath many trees on college lawns smelling rich with the scent of spring. For the next ten weeks, I'm here to use my graduate degrees to teach women about starting small businesses as a mechanism to alleviate poverty.

"And where will you stay?"

I tell her about my American friend who married a South African. "With them," I say.

She presses a new stamp against a fresh page, smiles as she slides my passport back to me, and says, "Maybe that will happen for you too."

I offer her a brief laugh, even though that idea holds little interest for me. The immigration officer can't know of the Alaska I now want more than all the cities and countries where I've lived. A place marked with the firm memories of the past that speak of where I think I want to be. The bountiful summer days. Even the harsh, still winter nights. The streets that curve past familiar landscapes of mountains and birch trees, bending and turning just as I've always known. The friends—the old family friends—who hug me and say, "We're so glad you're home." I've long forgotten the faint prayer for a son of Jamaican immigrants, someone with a background like mine.

I load my bags on the luggage cart and pass without fanfare or incident through customs. In the bright arrivals terminal where long windows let in views of grayish sky and parked planes, my friend's husband introduces me to his friend Nyasha, a man from Zimbabwe. Nyasha gives off a certain aura of one who makes his bed each morning and doesn't leave used cereal bowls in the kitchen sink but who, perhaps, also has a touch of whimsy hidden beneath all that I think I see. He smiles at me, the type of smile that makes use of his entire face, running from his dark eyes, through the rise of his cheeks and ending with a grin wide enough to give a generous welcome to this new place.

"Can you please write down your name?" I ask, sifting through my purse for a pen and paper, eager to say his name correctly and keep it implanted in my brain. Years later I will find that piece of paper and run my index finger over the slight indentation of six block letters and remember a breakfast at an airport café smelling of coffee and bacon, sausages and fried eggs. When we finish the meal, Nyasha takes one of my bags, my friend's husband the other, and then Nyasha drives us to my friend's home through that winter day, the splendor of Table Mountain bold in the backdrop and a hint of rain falling through the morning haze.

On another day, when Cape Town hides within a cloud of fog, I prepare a Jamaican meal for my friends and invite Nyasha to join us. This man who studied accounting and knows about business like me, who sometimes comes home with my friend's husband after attending a church meeting—I find I look forward to seeing him. He'll stay for dinner and talk with me about a recent article in the *Economist* or *Harvard Business Review*, and occasionally we'll speak of our shared faith and theology. For the Jamaican dinner, I season chicken parts with pepper and salt, thyme and slivers of onion too. I add coconut milk to red beans steaming together with rice. And I slice an avocado into slim wedges that I spiral around a plate in an artful design.

Later that evening we gather to eat in the living room, the dark and cold pressing with familiarity against the windows and the portable heater humming in the background. "Oh, avocado pears," Nyasha says after we pray and begin to feast on chicken soaked in gravy and served alongside traditional rice and peas.

"You call it that?" I ask, astonished. I think of the many years in Alaska when avocados sat on our kitchen counter, their skin turning dark and the meat inside softening to my mother's perfect ripe. "My parents call them pears too." And later that night, after I thank Nyasha for coming and wave goodbye, I smile when I remember that he called them pears, and I fully understood his meaning.

Even though a frail rain mists most days, leaving the air inside and out smelling damp, I plan a party at another friend's house in honor of my home country's Independence Day. A day to toss meat over flames and decorate a cake with red, white, and blue frosting. An excuse to gather and a time for me to celebrate.

"Do people exchange gifts on the Fourth of July?" Nyasha asks me this time. I tell him no, but on the way home from the party, both of us seated in his little blue car, he glances in my direction and says there's something for me in the glove compartment. It's a dark chocolate bar, tasting at once bitter and sweet. Months later, when his face is just a picture on my computer screen and my face a picture on his, when I sit in the chair in my mother's den and he travels to an

Internet cafe, we will talk about dark chocolate bars and independence days. "Bob Marley. He sang at Zimbabwe's first independence day," Nyasha will say. I'll watch a short clip of that moment, a fresh flag of green, yellow, red, black, and white hoisted high in the air, flying over a new country, and the smooth voice of a reggae singer ushering a crowd into celebration of freedom. Jamaican Bob Marley sang at Zimbabwe's independence day.

The night before I leave Cape Town, Nyasha picks me up near Table Bay Harbour after my day touring Robben Island. We wind our way back alongside Table Mountain to my friend's house, the sun setting over the ocean and early evening turning to twilight. I catch him looking for brief moments in my direction. The heat from the car warms my chilled fingers, and both of us know that tomorrow I will leave winter, fly for a day and a half, and enter the summer that awaits.

"Can I ask you a question?" he asks, continuing after I nod yes. "Do you consider yourself a practical person?" A band of moonlight falls across the car, allowing me to see the curve of his cheek, the crease in his forehead as he speaks. What I want to hear are all the words I imagine he could say: that space and distance are things of our imaginations, that the world is not a big place but a small one, that perhaps I don't really live so far away.

"No," I say. "I consider myself a dreamer, a person who believes in what can be and not what is."

So many years ago, on dark winter nights, I offered prayers for what I didn't even have words to say. A college campus across the country with broad, leafy trees. Cities with tube stops and afternoon tea. Someone to marry who was like me.

I fly home the next evening, up through the clouds, out of winter, into summer. In the dark plane cabin with a tiny light illuminating my tray table, I fill pages of my journal with thoughts of a

Zimbabwean living in South Africa and the way he promised to write me, the Jamaican American woman he hardly knows. There is space between me and him, there is an altering of my precise prayer, there is a compression of the globe that I could not have imagined. And there is all that came before and all that will come after.

I turn off the tiny overhead light and lean my head against the window. With my eyes closed, I drift back to Cape Town, finding my dreams remain in many ways the same.

Chapter 18

Marking the Color Trail

Spin, I hear my thoughts say. *Spin*. And so I do. My right foot steps away from my left, and I am a bride in motion. First one circle. Then another. On my wedding day, a breeze from an open window rustles my dress while smooth satin brushes my ankles. Peeking from under the swaying hemline is crimson nail polish framed by my brown skin. In a mirror I see something beyond bright lips turned up in a smile or the A-line silhouette spreading from my waist.

Spin again. As the skirt inflates and the current of air rushes against my bare legs, I know I look just as I had envisioned. Within seconds the dress descends to reality, the current disappears, and folds of soft fabric flit against my skin once more. A final look, then I reach for the bouquet of white calla lilies secured by a single scarlet ribbon. With my flowers in hand I approach an aisle dusted with rose petals.

~

Just days after my fiancé presented me with a bold blue sapphire for my ring finger, I hugged him beneath the bright-red digits of an airport clock. Until our wedding six months later, he would remain in Cape Town while I returned to the States. Twenty minutes after exiting security and ten minutes after clearing passport control, I rummaged through the magazine section of a bookstore. *A bride-to-be with a sixteen-hour flight ahead of her deserves a bridal magazine*, I reasoned.

As the plane accelerated down the runway and the wings cut through the clouds, I inhaled the sharp scent of fresh-cut paper. With each turn of the page I encountered dresses: formal, modern, princess, and ankle-length casual in white, off-white, cream, and the occasional ivory. After one last glance through the plane window at the rippled turquoise of the ocean, I stuffed the magazine into the seat pocket in front of me. My eyes closed. I was aware that the glossy pages couldn't offer what I had already envisioned.

One day at the train station in the suburbs of Cape Town, my South African coworker mentioned "beige children."

Just after graduate school, I had received a grant to work in a township on the outskirts of the city. As my time across the ocean dwindled, Minah and I sat waiting on a hard bench. A half hour stood between our seat on the platform and the inbound train to Muizenberg. She sipped a bottle of soda while I tore open a bag of corn chips. After a day spent helping women develop their business ideas, it would have been acceptable for the conversation to meander to lighter topics—perhaps a comment about Minah's love of cola or how chilly the afternoon felt. We could have even diverted the focus to the sweet Zimbabwean man I had met a few weeks earlier. In my daydreams I let myself think he was on the path to permanence in my life.

But after some time in Cape Town, I realized my classification as a black American unlocked certain conversations with black South

Africans. Today was no different. So with the wind blowing off the water beyond the station, we chatted about the fresh engagement of two acquaintances, a white woman and a black man.

"People celebrate such marriages as the new South Africa. How we cross cultures and create beige children. But I married outside my culture too," Minah said. I thought about her Xhosa heritage and marriage to a Sotho man.

Her annoyance made sense. In our small social group intercultural couples received a special nod, as if they had scaled a mountain of enlightenment. But I had noticed that "intercultural marriage" was a title bestowed on only those who fit the more obvious subcategory of "inter*racial* marriage." And the interracial marriages that merited conversation invariably involved a white person paired with someone of another race. Somehow the degree of difference between skin color became what determined how far couples ventured outside their individual identities.

Ten months later, on my two-week return visit to the Southern Hemisphere, the sweet Zimbabwean man proposed. As we stood mere feet from the edge of a cliff overlooking a suburb of Cape Town, my squeal of affirmation joined the strong wind around us. The glint of sunlight bouncing off the blue waves of the Atlantic soaking the beach below reminded me of the sapphire now heavy on my finger. As his hand reached for mine, I couldn't help but notice his skin, just a shade darker than my own.

$\sim$

Shortly after I arrived in Cape Town the first time, on the car ride back from a new friend's birthday lunch, she told me about "white weddings." The alliterative phrase piqued my interest.

"Well, versus lobola," Vuyi said in reference to traditional wedding ceremonies that people in several southern African countries practiced. "First, at the lobola ceremony, the family negotiates the bride price." She talked about how after this, the couple is traditionally considered married. Then days, weeks, or even months later, there could be a typical Western wedding—a "white wedding."

"It's complicated," she explained after I asked why people do both. "Some want an opportunity for a party. Others believe church weddings are more official. Perhaps some dream of spinning in a beautiful white dress."

Even as she spoke, I imagined the reach of Western culture extending like long fingers across continents. Black South African girls must have witnessed movies and television programs with fluffy white dresses and handsome grooms, just as I had as a young American girl. "White wedding" seemed like a nice way to package the Western trappings of nuptial bliss as if bridesmaids, a minister, a wedding march, and a white dress made a marriage. Only later did I consider that the word *white* might not have meant the wedding dress as I assumed. Perhaps it could have referenced the people who originated the custom.

The summer before graduate school, I shouted across the apartment to Jessica about the book I was reading on race and Christianity. For the few months before school began, I lived with her in the second-floor apartment on Garson Avenue in Rochester, New York. That lazy Saturday afternoon, while Jessica made herself tea, I sat in the living room with my legs curled up on the faded couch, turning the pages of the slim book.

"It's not just me." I raised my voice to reach her over the whistle of the kettle. "It's not just me," I said again before she could answer. "Metaphors about being 'washed white as snow' bother other people too." I pulled myself from the deep couch that threatened to suck me in. Our paths met at the edge of the kitchen, where her pink hands wrapped around a large mug. "It's just that sometimes all this talk about being made white as snow, all the images of being black with sin before cleansing makes us white—sometimes it's just a lot. . . ."

My voice trailed off. I held the book before her, offering it as if the words could rise up and articulate what I was stumbling through. I wanted to explain to her the weariness of knowing the name for the color of one's skin equates with evil, sin, and death. I wanted to talk about faultless colors shoved in hierarchical structures, but I just said, "The color white gets tiring."

She nodded her head as if she understood. And I think she did.

A few months into my junior year abroad, the day after my friends and I ate one of our many dinners at the Indian restaurant down the road from the Bayswater tube station, I found an empty seat in the student computer lab. The spicy masala had faded into my memory, but the previous evening's conversation had left me curious.

On keys faded and worn from hundreds of papers typed and computer programs written, my fingers tapped out a query: "History white wedding dresses." My brain absorbed a pile of new information about what I had considered an ancient tradition. And why not? White wedding dresses felt as traditional as diamond engagement rings—which I soon learned were both about as ancient as the nineteenth century.[1] After an hour at the computer, I felt as if I was unearthing some conspiracy plan to either equate white with goodness and purity or, at least, to dress all the world's brides in the same color.

A single year: 1840.

A single wedding: between Britain's Queen Victoria and Prince Albert, her in lacy white.

At first, I assumed Queen Victoria had picked white to flaunt her chastity, as if to cloak herself in her own virginity. A few websites later I realized she might have been a queen, but on her wedding day she was first a bride. Modern brides turn a favorite necklace, flower, or season into the theme of an entire wedding, and Queen Victoria was no different. The inspiration for her white dress came from a desire to use a certain lace.[2] And a century and a half later, the West and so many parts of the rest of the world adhered to the tradition like an eleventh commandment. Even I felt pressure to adhere to a rule not originating in my own culture.

Thank you, Queen Victoria. And thank you, imperialism.

The evening my friends and I ate dinner at the Indian restaurant down the road from the Bayswater tube station, Shamik mentioned that brides in India get married in red. Over a table full of chicken tikka masala, saag paneer, and dahl, flanked on either end by steaming baskets of naan, he explained a tradition I had never heard of despite my own family ties to India. How the conversation emerged, I'm uncertain. There were enough barely twenty-year-old women at the table, myself included, who could have hijacked any discussion and lured it to the topic of weddings.

As Shamik continued his explanation, my thoughts wandered to Hester's scarlet letter back in high school English, to femme fatales with bright red lipstick, and to Eve reaching for a perfect crimson apple. I heard Shamik's voice, but only snippets of his explanation reached my ears: passion, joy, commitment.

As the discussion continued, my fingers sopped up bits of the savory, spicy curry with a piece of naan. Occasionally I saw vibrant red-orange streaks of masala painting the cloth napkin I used.

Could red really be a bridal color?

It is after church one Sunday, and I am perhaps three or four. I stand behind my mother's leg as she speaks with a friend in the foyer of what will later be my high school. My church lacks a building of its own, so we meet in a school, in classrooms that will one day be my chemistry class or my calculus class or my world history class—"world history," which really is just a euphemism for European history from the ancient Greeks until just before World War II. We walk through hallways where I will one day be the rare black student in the snow-colored landscape of faces sprawling around me.

But at three or perhaps four, I press against my mother's leg, wearing a red-checkered dress, my matching red tights, and bright red shoes. As I wait for my mother, I think of the immense twirling power hidden in the soft folds of my clothes.

My mother's friend turns to me and comments on my beauty. Being reminded of a truth I somehow know, her words compel my mouth to smile, my body to shift away from my mother, and my right foot to accelerate me into motion. A blur of bright red fabric rises around me, and without knowing, I spin myself into a reflection of my wedding day.

Chapter 19

Before

The day I prepare to lay my daughter to nap on her great-grandmother's bed, I think, *I have been here before.* Outside the air is warm like a breath in my cupped hands. Past the front door, a dense fog blinds me to the landscape beyond as the call of a rooster joins the rustle of leaves cloaking thick trees. In this cramped corner room I know I have seen this mattress snug against a wall. I have watched light from the small window pierce a dark room.

But, of course, this day is my first time in this hidden pocket of rural Zimbabwe. It is the day my daughter is introduced to her great-grandmother, my husband's grandmother.

I have been here before. I have stood by this bed—and not this bed. Here—and not here. In a clearing through the trees. Through the secret passage between bowing branches. In this small home. In these rural areas. Not these rural areas.

Rural Jamaica. Not a clearing through the trees but the top of a mountain. An introduction to a grandmother I don't know.

I look up to a high bed, my grandmother's bed. *How does she sleep up there,* I wonder. *How does she climb in bed?* There is a light from the window, the small window just above where the mattress meets the wall. The afternoon sun casts streaks of gold across the dim. Someone's arms lift me. My worn-out body is placed on the crisp, tight sheets. Even in the cool room, the heavy air and low voices nearby feel like the warmth of a soft blanket.

As my bare arms rub against the smooth bed, I turn to the side and curl my knees toward my chest. I drift toward sleep, thankful to be inside as heat bears down beyond the door. For the length of a nap, perhaps the length of a day, I am part of what blows through rural Jamaican leaves on top of this mountain.

In Zimbabwe my daughter sleeps in my arms with her body curved into my side. Her chest inflates and deflates in a rhythmic cycle while soft sleep breath tickles my shoulder. Beside where I stand is the bed she will soon rest on.

I don't remember the climb up the mountain, the fragrant scent of tropical flowers saturating the air, the symphony of songbirds warbling in the trees. I can't taste the rainwater from the heavy drum, dribbling down my mouth, cool like metal. And in my mind my grandmother remains without a face.

My daughter won't remember the tears of dew rolling off bright leaves or the cows sinking slightly into the damp ground. She won't recall sitting at her great-grandmother's feet while leather fingers crush thin peanut shells. Her great-grandmother's song that welcomed us to this rural home will elude her.

The clap of footsteps on the concrete floor breaks the quiet, and someone spreads a woven blanket across the bed. The strands of wool dive over and under each other as if racing to the worn edge. They lock together to form the tight weave that will separate my toddler from her great-grandmother's bare mattress. Even as I pull her from my shoulder and place her body against the scratchy surface, her eyes remain closed. My wrists flick a baby blanket in the air, and a breeze runs across her body before the weight of warmth settles against her skin.

Is this where longing begins? The desire for passports streaked with stamps. A yearning for cities that become temporary homes. A fake love of skyscrapers and fast planes. Will she also one day take walks through cities with perfect grids and hope for bends in rustic roads? Will unfinished books gather on her nightstand as she stares at rivers with tangled currents moving to some vast unknown? I think this is the birthplace of searching, a searching for something that is lost before we can even remember. Crisp sheets, humid air, the feel of woven blankets beneath us. A searching that doesn't diminish with a generation but likely grows and grows until it encompasses the breadth and depth of the world.

I stare at her asleep on the blanket. The sunlight crawls across the bed, parting the room's shadows. Wait, no. Beyond this window a drizzle coats the ground, burdens the air. A gray light. Yes, a gray light grazes the dim and reveals her face.

I think perhaps one day her dreams will unlock this bed, this window, this moment. If nothing more, perhaps she will remember a mattress pushed against the wall and a small window that ushers in light.

Perhaps she will say she has been here before.

Chapter 20

Braided Love

My baby girl sits on the bathroom counter, body facing the mirror, hands grabbing at hair elastics, a bottle of lotion, or whatever else is in reach. I drape the towel over her shoulders and unravel her braids, now fuzzy from toddler life. Every girl with hair like my daughter's or mine experiences the beginnings of this type of hair routine. Our coiled strands stretch in multiple directions, sprouting from our heads like the proud branches of a mighty tree with roots extending to Jamaica, India, and parts of the African continent. Our hair relies on tender care: gentle shampoos, thick conditioners, oil to add moisture, wide-toothed combs. I massage coconut oil into these dense locks and use the comb to prepare her hair for four braids, anticipating the beginning of her tears.

And the tears come.

Not immediately, though. First her palms press against her head and prevent my comb from pulling the tangled strands. I move with caution while I hum nursery rhymes to quiet her antsy body. Each time we settle into this process, I'm tempted to leave the strands loose and free. But if I choose that route, I know a fight with major tangles

155

looms, one that will result in her hysterical screams, her pleading eyes, and perhaps the possibility of having to cut the resistant snags. For a not-yet-two-year-old and her timid mother, it's much easier to face the slight challenges of detangling and retwisting hair back into the shape of braids.

I work through the ends, moving upward to the root, and sometimes, when I reach a particularly knotted lock, she jerks her head away, her eyes start to flood, and I'm forced to begin again. Frustration is building inside me. Braiding will decrease the accumulation of knots, but I wish combing the tangles didn't hurt her. I wish the process were easier. I wish I possessed greater skill. What message am I communicating as I tug and pull at her hair? Can a toddler sense affection in the mother who brings her pain?

"All done, baby girl. You look lovely!"

Her eyes meet her reflection in the glass. They brighten and match her unfolding smile, her lips touching the mirror in a self-kiss that declares her image beautiful. As I watch, I try to remember a time when my own child-self adored the face staring back at me. A time before I became dissatisfied with my appearance, long before I found peace in the sight of my reflection once again.

But I can't. In all my memories of childhood, nothing about my appearance brought me contentment. Not my shape. Not my complexion. Not the hair my mother braided each day.

~

My mother had a sweet, floral scent from the special lotion on her bathroom counter. This aroma, combined with the strong smell of hair oil, tickled my nose while I sat in front of her on the stool beside her bed. One by one she untwisted my braids. Morning after morning, year after year, my mother combed and braided my hair while I stared into the mirror hanging on her bedroom wall.

I can't recall all that occurred between us in those moments. We had conversations, of course. Perhaps about spelling words or friendships. There was talk of chores, I'm sure. What I remember, though, is my mother braiding my hair with precision, knowledge, speed, and resolve. Even in the midst of a busy morning, she made time to unravel, brush, and rebraid. It would be years before I comprehended the message this act imparted. As a child, though, I stared into the mirror, unsatisfied.

The mirror reminded me that my braids looked nothing like the streamers of hair flowing through my classroom at school. Every girl there seemed to have hair as straight as the lines on my notebook paper. I wanted that hair. Mine was the single black face amid the white in my class photos, but it was my hair that drew the attention.

To the amazement of my classmates, my braids had the power to hold their shape without the aid of pesky elastics. To my humiliation, when several girls declared that people like me put oil in their hair, I had to admit they were right. I wanted to explain why. I wanted them to understand. But their repulsed expressions made me keep silent.

Each curious comment was further proof that my hair wouldn't fit the smooth strands celebrated in nearly every direction I turned. I watched the same animated movie princesses with their pale skin and abundant hair. I flipped through the same magazines with the stark absence of girls who looked like me. "No one wears braids like this," I said to my mother. "No one. I just wish my hair were different." Those braids were thick arrows that each day pointed to my failure to meet the standards of beauty floating through my life.

Just after my eleventh birthday, my mother agreed to let me exchange my coiled mass for chemically straightened hair. She abandoned our daily braiding sessions and embraced blow dryers and curling irons instead. With my straightened hair flowing past my shoulders and my index finger tucking loose strands behind my ears, I knew I'd found the beginnings of happiness with my hair.

Over the next eleven years I tried bangs, bone-straight hair, hot curlers, and even layers, like the women in the sitcom *Friends*. My hair traveled the gamut of styles as time passed and my world expanded to include more women who looked like me. Late one evening toward the end of college, I found myself staring in the mirror again. By now I used the word *beautiful* to describe the curve of my hips and the soft angles of my face and the medium brown of my skin. *This is who I am*, I told myself. *And who I am is good.*

The straight hair I saw in the mirror burdened me. I'd been feeling unsettled and weary with my hair for months. Maybe I was exhausted from using chemicals to force my hair into something it wasn't. Or perhaps I was tired of the constant prompting to ensure my hair looked a certain way.

I reached for the cold curling iron and touched the metal that had curled my straightened hair year after year. I raised my hands to my head and ran my fingers through my smooth mane. As I stood there, looking in the mirror as I'd done so many times before, a verse fragment reverberated in my mind. *Fearfully and wonderfully made. Fearfully and wonderfully made.* I breathed out a long sigh. The very hair I'd spent so many years wanting reminded me of the synthetic material that framed a doll's face.

In that moment of surrender I understood something I hadn't grasped before: my faith invited me to see myself as part of divine creation. I wouldn't find peace by changing my appearance. So after years of striving for another look, I wanted my curves, my complexion—and my hair. It was time to revert to my naturally springy coils. And my mother was still there, willing to help braid.

My daughter and I visit my mother's home where it's been years since she last braided hair, but the hair accessories I remember remain. Perhaps my mother misses those morning braiding sessions. Or maybe she saves the brush and hair bands as tributes to daughters now grown. More likely, though, she keeps them in the hope—now fulfilled—of little-girl feet running though her house once again.

Our first morning home, my mother spreads a towel over part of her bed to protect the heavy comforter. She sets my daughter on the towel and stands behind her, unraveling her braids. She massages oil into the strands, just as I've done in the past. I watch my mother brush, part, and braid my daughter's coils as if she were a fragile figurine. My little girl's tears fall for my mother the way they do for me, but I notice my mother's confidence. I study her technique, trying to learn how to make this process easier for my daughter and for me.

My mother mists a leave-in conditioner over my daughter's hair and uses the brush to create even parts. I see the tenderness in her able hands that communicates a deep love for the little girl seated on her bed. My mother's fingers say that my daughter is worth the time and worth the effort, that she is loved. This is same message my mother's fingers told me each morning of my childhood. Her desire to ensure my even parts and neat braids were her way of teaching me to see beauty and worth in my reflection—even if I questioned that truth.

Later in the day my mother and I sit on her couch and clutch mugs of tea. Stillness fills the house as my daughter naps in my old bedroom. While we sip our drinks, my mother's words meander through her stories of raising daughters. Sometimes, my mother tells me, she expected me to understand what she was trying to teach through her actions alone. Now, she confesses, she wishes she had augmented those lessons with words and spoken what she wanted to convey.

I think back to a few hours before, to when I watched my daughter perched on my mother's bed. My mother's regrets make me consider what I hope to teach my own daughter as I unravel her braids. Perhaps it isn't enough for me to set aside time for her hair. The act of applying oil to her scalp and twisting her strands into braids may only whisper a message I want her to hear, a whisper she won't discern until she has the maturity to silence the cacophony of opinions ringing in every woman's ears.

I envision the years ahead as I develop greater precision and skill. When my daughter sits in front of me and stares at her reflection, I will do more than braid. I'll add words to the message my mother taught me. As one braiding session folds into the next, I will tell stories of the rich heritage in every strand of my daughter's hair. With each gentle tug at her tangles, I'll tell her that her curls form part of divine creation. The words I share and the time I give my daughter will remind a baby, then a child, then a woman that she, too, is loved. Not because of what she looks like but because she is a created being.

I will part her hair into three sections. As I twist each strand, I will speak of my mother, my daughter, and me: three generations entwined, passing along a message of love through the simplicity of braided hair.

Chapter 21

Holding On

"It reminds me of Zimbabwe," Nyasha says as he stares out the car window at the changing landscape of Jamaica's northeastern coast. Trees with lush, green leaves fringe the two-lane road. Peeking through the swaying palms, we see a cobalt sea. A current of air passes between Nyasha's rolled-down window and mine, and I taste salt in the air when my lips part into a smile. "Except the sea," he adds. "Zimbabwe doesn't have the sea."

My uncle navigates the car past a settlement—too small to be called a town—on our way to the resort where Nyasha and I will soon wed. In the backseat my fingers are laced in Nyasha's and rest against his khaki shorts. Through the window I see little shops and stands selling ripe plantains and fresh breadfruit. Ahead of us hordes of school children in uniforms flock near the edge of the road. Their neatly pressed skirts and trousers make me imagine a Zimbabwe I have never seen.

"The children. The uniforms. It's just like home," he says. We hear the laughter of youth catch the breeze and curl into the air. I think Nyasha sees a Jamaica I imagine I know, a place my parents speak of as their first home. Our fingers still entwined, I glance at the engrossed expression on Nyasha's face and squeeze his hand, already sweaty from the humid air. The scent of my parents' island floats through the open window, and I smile at Nyasha's comfort in a place he has never been. He still knows this place, and perhaps I do too.

Nyasha and I begin our marriage in South Africa. The place where we first met, we both now call home.

Back in 2007, he had been living in South Africa for more than six years and was a few months away from becoming a chartered accountant. I had short-term plans for my time in Cape Town. Teach some students. Conduct some research. Complete the requirements of a grant.

The day I arrived, though, I met Nyasha.

"Oh, love at first sight," people say with a dreamy expression. But I'm honest, and I don't weave stories that don't exist. Not love. Not love at first. But something. And that something became something more until the day in my parents' homeland on top of a small cliff when we faced each other and made weighty promises about a life we couldn't yet know. The foamy surf beat against the shore below, salty waves soaking the beach before shrinking back into the wide sea.

~

Can a name mark a child? Can it whisper to her of distant roads and horizon dotted with acacia trees? Can it speak of the places from which she descends? I must think so because I insist on a name from Nyasha's language for the child growing inside of me. I imagine when our plans return us to America, as I know they one day will, a Shona name will stretch across the ocean, binding our daughter to a

Zimbabwe she may never know. Nyasha just wants a name we like, so he doesn't mind the way I ask again and again for more Shona names.

After dinner I relax on our bed. Nyasha kneels on the floor with his elbows sinking into the duvet. Here we talk of the day, and I listen for Shona names to slip from my husband's conversation. Later that evening, or perhaps another so similar I think them all the same, the slightest flutter taps me from the inside. From where the newspaper spreads across his side of the bed, Nyasha reads an article about a Zimbabwean woman named Sekai.

"*Sekai* means laughter," he says.

I fall asleep to butterfly kicks and a name to mark a child.

A year after Sekai's birth, Nyasha and I stand in front of a counter at the US embassy. I hold Sekai against my hip and watch Nyasha pull a stack of our wedding pictures from a manila envelope. He slides the photographs beneath the gap between window and countertop into the waiting hands of the embassy employee. She flips through the images from not quite two years before—the bright smiles on Nyasha's face and mine, the seafoam color of water rolling behind us on a Jamaican beach. Sekai grows antsy, and I shift her to my other hip as I try to catch a glimpse of the photographs. Do we grin widely enough? Do our expressions exhibit sufficient happiness that there is no doubt as to the reality of our love?

"We have our letters too," I offer as we wait for a stranger to declare our marriage legitimate and grant Nyasha a US immigration visa. My free hand reaches for the pile of letters Nyasha and I exchanged before our wedding.

"No, no." She shakes her head. "This is fine."

Later, when Nyasha touches the new visa plastered against a page in his passport, he asks, "Where should we go?"

I reach for a gauzy memory of a magazine article, a handful of words I once read about boundless opportunities in a city I'd never seen. Charlotte, North Carolina. Mild winters compared to Anchorage. A place that could be a good compromise in distance between my Alaskan birthplace and Nyasha's Zimbabwean homeland.

"Perhaps Charlotte," I say, a suggestion that becomes a reality.

Four hours after we leave my mother-in-law's home in Gweru, we drive into a small pocket of rural Zimbabwe. When we began our journey, the dawn hadn't yet shaken off the shadows of night. Now we arrive in humble Wedza under a gray blanket of drizzle and fog—so much fog I can't even see the large hills my husband later tells me meet the sky.

We come to this place to say our goodbyes as we prepare to move to Charlotte. From the corner of Nyasha's grandmother's home, I watch Sekai press her body prostrate against a cement floor. Her raised head stares beyond the open door to where two chickens skip across the land. I move to stand behind her with my camera. Her face now hidden from view, I imagine the crease of a smile shaping her mouth. Perhaps she wants to do more than watch. As the chickens glide through the drizzle, I think her unseen expression might reveal a longing to reach out and grab hold.

In the months and years to come, as our family makes America our home, I will frame this photograph and say to my daughter time and time again, "That's you there. That's you in Zimbabwe looking at your great-grandmother's chickens. That's you." I will tell her about the misty rain hovering over the earth and the way Nyasha's grandmother lifted her from the car with a joyful song. I will say these things so she can feel the cold concrete through her clothes and against her flattened palms. In her dreams I want her to hear the sounds of the rooster crowing and the tree branches rustling. I want her to taste fine drops of rain on her tongue. So I will tell her this story, believing that one day she will walk down a narrow path in her father's land and hear a voice whisper her name.

For more than the first few years of our new life in Charlotte, there are thorns. Thorns that wound our palms and puncture our flesh when we grab at the dream of this new place.

"I'm sorry," I say to Nyasha late one night that could be many nights as I stare at his crumpled shoulders. I say these words when I think of the friends he had in Cape Town, the job he liked, the family he left behind on the other side of a vast ocean. He reaches for both of my hands, and together our arms make a circle that for a moment cannot break.

And in the middle of these years, we welcome another child into our family. We take her Shona name from a song. "Shamiso," Nyasha tells me. "It means miracle."

Nyasha holds her against his chest and moves back and forth and side to side, pressing figure eights into the carpet. He croons, "Shami. Shami. Shamiso," as he tilts his face toward her head of dark curls.

We link her life to a place she's never been. We name her for the miracle she is. We name her for the miracles I hope will come.

"Motsi, piri, tatu, china." From the bathroom where I bathe baby Shamiso, I hear Sekai in her bedroom, counting in Shona. She and Nyasha read a book I ordered online called *Count Your Way through Zimbabwe*. Sekai learns to count to ten, and I develop visions of Sekai speaking Nyasha's language. Isn't that what parents do? They teach their children their languages.

"But, Patrice," Nyasha will tell me later, "I don't really speak Shona. I speak English."

He's right of course. Before we married, we shared dinner with several friends, many of them speakers of multiple languages. Everyone else spent the evening talking of how one must hold on to language. How we must teach these things to our children so they don't lose their culture, so it doesn't spill from their hands and disappear beyond their reach. Again and again others emphasized the importance of retaining who we are and not letting dominant cultures overshadow our inherited pasts. And I believed the words they spoke.

Toward the end of the evening, Nyasha set down the plate of cake he held and said, "I speak English. I know Shona, but I speak English. I say, 'good morning' to each new day. 'Mangwanani' never enters my mind."

The room quieted as he picked up his plate once more, brought another bite of cake to his mouth, and asked, "What is culture? Who decides what we keep?"

Sekai repeats the numbers to ten again. "Gumi," she says a final time before Nyasha pulls the covers to her chin, prays for her, and switches out the light. He leaves the book behind.

Sometimes I imagine phantoms. As if voices whisper in my ears and feed fears that my American culture eclipses all that makes my husband Zimbabwean. All that makes him Shona. *Because of you, your husband's ties to his country will become flabby. Because of you, your children will be called visitors in their father's first home.*

"Where do the voices come from?" Nyasha asks me when I try to explain shapeless ideas that hide in my mind.

"People," I say. The people who ask me why Nyasha doesn't teach the girls to speak Shona. The Zimbabwean man and his mother we ran into at the local museum, and I realized I hadn't heard Nyasha speak Shona since we'd moved to the States. The friends we know in cross-cultural marriages with children fluent in other tongues.

"People," I repeat. Can such a general word give flesh to what gnaws at my ears?

"Me?" he asks. He points his index finger at his chest and stares at my face. I see his broad nose, his dark skin, and his deep brown eyes that warm me on the coldest of days.

I shake my head. "No. Not you. Never you." He lifts his hand and settles it on my shoulder, reminding me of what we create together.

~

My mother sometimes speaks of loss. Of music. Of language. Of what makes her Jamaican. Of what she should have passed on to her children. Each time she visits the island, she calls from my uncle's home in Kingston or from her hotel room overlooking pristine sand in Montego Bay and says, "Patrice, I'm moving back."

She never does.

On another day she sits near me while we fold laundry on the living room floor. The smell of detergent and fresh clothes makes the air sweet and comfortable. In these soft moments that allow for one to inhale deep breaths and reflect on all that has gone by, my mother might say, "We should have tried harder to hold on to things," speaking of both herself and my father.

I grab Shamiso's pajamas or Sekai's socks and fold them. "Hold on to what?"

"To Jamaican things," she says. I think of Sunday meals of brown stew chicken served alongside rice and peas. I traipse in memory back to our kitchen table and the scotch bonnet peppers my father fished from a jar of vinegar while I sifted through my rice and removed each and every pea. And there was more. So much more. The slow-cooked oxtail, the curried chicken, the fried dumplings, the rotis. As these images move through my mind, savory aromas compete with the smell of clothes I hold. For a moment I straddle memory and the present and crave dishes I haven't eaten in years.

"But you cooked food. So much food."

"No. Not the food. Other things." She talks of songs and sayings, the way one's tongue can curl around a patwa phrase. She speaks of culture. Of passing down customs and traditions beyond Easter bun and beef patties.

I sit in my living room in Charlotte and remember when my mother and I traveled to Jamaica a few months after Nyasha and I met. My third trip in a lifetime. We woke early one morning and journeyed to the foot of a small mountain. Before us a narrow trail twisted ahead, flanked on both sides by a thick covering of trees. Tiny dewdrops hung on leaves while the sun began to slide higher in the sky. Woven in with the sound of our footsteps, the whistle of birds continued to call forth the morning. We moved toward the top of this mountain—really a hill—as light crept across the path, the trees, even my bare arms. The smell of damp earth, the bold tang of bright flowers, the scent of spicy bushes ushered in a new day. As I pressed forward, I imagined for a moment the sound of my name rustled through branches. A song of welcome from another home.

I hear what my mother says. It's not just about food but also culture and music, phrases and sayings. But I think of how, in the absence of so much else, I still pronounce *plantain* with a short *i* sound instead of a long *a*—just like other Jamaicans. I remind myself that the smooth sound of reggae makes my hips sway. I think of all that I do know.

~⁀

"Both my father's eldest brother and my mother's uncle studied in the States," Nyasha mentions to me one night after we put the girls to bed. He has told these stories before. They have flitted in and around our conversations from our beginning. But now I stop and ask again about Nyasha's uncle. About Nyasha's great-uncle.

You come from people who move, I think and imagine the world compressing from continents into paths that people walk across from Zimbabwe to America. From America to South Africa. From Zimbabwe to South Africa. From Jamaica to America.

He comes from people who move, I think over and over again that night when I brush my teeth, pull on my pajamas, press my cold feet against Nyasha's calves. I wonder how I didn't hear him. How I missed that.

I thought I knew what a Shona man was. I thought I knew all the things he believed he needed to keep. Was it possible that all along I saw an empty idea and missed the fullness of this man?

I think of my own immigrant parents and how their ancestors were taken to the shore of Jamaica in mighty boats after months bobbing along the sea. We both come from people who move across bodies of water and continents. We come from people who shed things and acquire things and then shed more. Accents. Languages. Food. Nationalities.

The things we overlook when we think we understand.

For the length of Nyasha's American citizenship ceremony, I hold both girls. Sekai and I share the final seat in the front row, and Shamiso sits on my lap. One arm secures Shamiso against me. The other drapes around Sekai's shoulder, preventing her from sliding off the chair. We stay like this while on the other side of the aisle Nyasha recites his oath with the eighty other naturalized citizens. When he walks across the front of the room to receive his certificate, my arms tighten around the girls.

In the final minutes of the ceremony, the lights flicker off, and we sit in a room of darkness. A video plays of the many faces of America—people born in this country and naturalized citizens from the far reaches of the world. The girls begin to squirm, anxious to move their legs and be free from my tight grip.

"Just another minute," I breathe. "Just another minute, and I can let you go." I hold Sekai's shoulder, but in an effort to prevent a cry, I set Shamiso on the floor near my feet. As the lights turn on in the room, the weight of my arm falls from Sekai to the chair.

"Okay, you can go. Take your sister to the corner so we can take pictures."

Sekai walks with Shamiso toward the floor-length American flags hanging in a tapestry of red, white, and blue. After being wrapped in my arms for so long, the empty space stretches before them. And I think perhaps all that *I* am summons me to grant them this release. Sekai grabs Shamiso's hands, and laughter spreads across their faces as they twirl in wide circles.

Chapter 22

Preparation Days

When I'm still a girl growing up in Anchorage, my mother and I spend a Saturday before Easter Sunday in preparation. Outside the snowdrifts shrink, melting icicles shatter against the driveway, and each day new patches of the green lawn appear—all signs that spring is near, but not quite here. Inside, though, we travel to my mother's Jamaican homeland. In our Alaskan kitchen, she shows me how to prepare a potato salad much like she made as a girl in Kingston. While I watch, my mother fills a pot with water, adds several eggs, and sets it to boil on the stove. Once the bubbles begin to pop in rapid succession, she slides peeled chunks of potatoes beneath the hot liquid, and we wait.

"It's easier to boil the potatoes with the eggs," she explains.

Later we spread the potatoes across a cookie sheet and let them cool. My mother takes a knife to the pieces too large for our liking as I crack and peel the eggs. She then pours frozen peas over the warm food. "The easiest way to defrost them," she says, and the cold of winter again meets the warmth of spring.

"Pepper and a little salt," she says, while we continue to work.

She tells me a story about her faraway girlhood in Jamaica and the class trip when she brought the potato salad. "I forgot to add the salt." She laughs as she sprinkles a pinch across the food, and I slice pickles down to the right size. "We ended up throwing it away."

I laugh too. Her story and her instructions draw me into a gauzy, feather-soft, muted longing, a state of being that conforms well to neatly pressed dresses, an anticipated Easter sunrise, and that great triumph now a day away.

Finally we pour everything into the bowl and add great clouds of mayonnaise before folding the ingredients together. "At Christmas you should make mashed potatoes," my mother says. "At Easter we lighten things up. We serve more salads." She gives me a rule to keep close, that potato salad is lighter fare, that Easter carries with it a certain airiness, a celebration that the weight of death has resurrected to life, elevating a simple side dish to something more.

My mother slides the potato salad into the refrigerator, ready for the next day. Tomorrow my family will gather around the heavy wooden table, pastel colors clothing my sister and me, the fragments of winter receding to the promise of spring. Before we pile our plates full with food, we will link our hands, bow our heads, and give thanks for the risen Christ.

~

The first Christmas Eve that Nyasha and I are married, I make a potato salad. We live in Cape Town, the near tip of the African continent, and the sun rises early each December morning only to droop late in the evening hours. During the lengthy daylight, a dense heat drapes the city, ripe with the smell of blossoms and budded life. A Cape Town summer. Here I can't imagine whipped potatoes with cream and butter, served hot in celebration of the Christmas season, so I plan for chilled side dishes, for salads blended with cold mayonnaise. I spend the morning in preparation, boiling eggs, pouring frozen peas over warm potatoes, sliding the finished salad into my refrigerator, ready for the next day.

The sun sinks below the horizon, and fresh evening air floats into our bedroom. The darkness delivers us from the intensity of the day. After Nyasha switches off the bedside lamp, we can see granules of stars in the black sky. And there are voices, voices riding the wind, traveling from where, I can't say, but voices sing in a sacred dark. "O Come All Ye Faithful." "Away in a Manger." "Silent Night."

I climb from where I sit on the bed and move closer to the distant melodies. I lean my head out the window into the soft sky. This night, perhaps this night, without piles of snow and crystals of ice, without frost-dusted pine trees and mugs of warm cider, perhaps this mild night and its subtle breeze recalls Bethlehem and a first Christmas so long ago.

My eyes strain in search of a gathering of people, of the flicker of candles burning yellow flames. Or perhaps I'll glimpse the radiance of angels bearing great halos of holy light. Nyasha joins me at the open window and tucks his arm around my waist. After a moment he pulls me near. Together we stare in the direction of sound rippling across invisible waves. "Sleep in heavenly peace," we sing together with the hushed pageantry of strangers.

Sleep in heavenly peace.

After we move to Charlotte, Nyasha, Sekai, and I spend a Christmas Eve with our Jamaican neighbors. When we enter the home, I smell the aromas of my childhood—the slight fragrance of coconut, the gentle scent of curry seasoning, the evidence of Jamaican food prepared within these walls.

We gather around the dinner table, and a bowl of potato salad sits with the other dishes. *But it's winter. But it's cold,* I think for a moment when I see a Jamaican live a different rule than the one my mother taught me. But I push aside my momentary surprise and take a serving: the confluence of boiled egg yolk and mayonnaise, the hint of salt coating the potato. It tastes just like the salad that I know.

Beyond the back window the day has turned to ink, and along the wall my neighbors display their many Christmas cards filled with shepherds, wise men, and foil stars. As we eat familiar food and share stories with new friends, images of babies in mangers and a multitude of heavenly hosts merge into thoughts of spring lilies and empty tombs.

Of course, of course, I think. The rules were never rules after all. Seated in that December darkness, I have seen a great light.

Chapter 23

What Remains

Just off Central Avenue they're tearing down Eastland Mall—the dead mall as I like to call it. Bulldozers and cranes cluster near broken concrete and piles of rubble.

In the beginning I saw the front of the building removed, the insides exposed like a little girl's dollhouse. As the rubble grew, I wondered if between the dust and crushed walls a lone hanger could be found, a pair of new shoes, or perhaps a going-out-of-business sign. Do dead malls hold on to any of that?

"Mommy, what are they doing?" my preschool-aged daughter asks from the backseat. My throat tightens. In an uncharacteristic neutral voice, I explain the demolition of the empty building and the city's desire for something new. Given Sekai's keen sense of observation, I wonder if she notices how I stare when we drive this block of Central. How can I explain to her my desire to stop the car and bury my head in my hands when I can't even explain this to myself? Who cries over a mall?

As a recent arrival to Charlotte, I never knew the dead mall when it was alive with the hum of eager shoppers and squalling children.

I never walked through the stores and touched soft fabrics or sifted through piles of sale CDs. I never sipped lemonade while middle schoolers exchanged first kisses just beyond the food court. I don't know what it was to circle and circle around bright green trees in search of an elusive parking spot. Still, I keep driving by, watching the demolition of a mall I never knew. A few more weeks and the dead mall will be a wasteland of concrete. Hundreds and thousands of parallel and perpendicular lines will provide parking for nothing. Not even an abandoned building.

What happens each day off Central makes me think of my hometown. A few blocks from Anchorage's local college is the University Center—or, to be more accurate, my own dead mall. Mine. As in the theater where I watched movies with high school friends I no longer know. The stores where I spent my babysitting money on books, cheap jewelry, and the occasional hair scrunchie. The studio where my family posed for one of our final portraits before the divorce. My dead mall.

I'm not sure anyone else—my parents or my sister—remembers that day near the back entrance by the movie theater. Still dressed in our church clothes, we walked through the doors as the smell of liquid butter coating stale popcorn flooded my nose and my sister's high heels tapped the tiled floor on the way to the studio. That family portrait remains among the last, frozen smiles—mother, father, and two girls.

Did my parents allow their fingers to entwine with each other's when I stopped to look at the comics in the bookstore? Did my father's face shine with pride as the sun's rays streamed through the skylight and streaked his wife and daughters' coordinated spring dresses?

Does it matter that perhaps no one remembers the photo, except me?

A few hours before dawn the baby's hiccupped cries shake me from my dreams. Before I can shrug off the weight of sleep, the mattress creaks as my husband rolls out of bed, and his bare feet pad across the carpeted floor. He brings Shamiso back to me, where I fall asleep nursing her. Both of us too tired to return her to the crib, she's still there when the door handle turns and Sekai shuffles toward us with a blanket dragging behind. She says, "Mommy, I can't sleep." As I drift back to sleep, she climbs onto the foot of the bed.

A few hours later, when the blue-black shadows of night dissolve into day, we remain there with our bodies brushing against one another. Shamiso sleeps between Nyasha and me, and Sekai is perpendicular to our feet. The stuffy smell of sleep sweat wakens me, and my baby's thumb touches my nose. Lying there, I wish the sun would forget for a moment its command to climb higher in the sky and let me stay here, near my family, forever.

When my sister and I were small, the dark of night and the quiet of the house made us tiptoe toward our parents' bedroom. We crept down the hallway in our pajamas, knocked softly, and pressed our faces to the slit between frame and door. In low voices we said, "We're scared. Can we come in?" Then came the click of the knob turning, and my sister and I piled into the warm bed.

Back when I used to whisper to my parents in the middle of the night, could they have guessed that the light in their marriage would dim and they would clutch regret surrounded by their crumbled dreams? When the morning sun sneaked through the blinds, and

they saw their daughters resting next to them, could they have predicted that what they had wasn't the kind of structure to survive a
generation?

$$\sim$$

*It's senior year of high school, and I lie on my bed with an open book
in front of me. The radio on my nightstand spits out one pop song after
another, and I hum along, a disconnected soundtrack for the plot unfolding in my book. Beyond my closed door, my father's sharp tone and raised
voice disrupt my reading trance. My mother's cries muffle her response
before I can make them out. And then I am not on my bed, the book tossed
on the floor where the cheap pages display their frailty against the carpet.
On the middle stair, I stand between the volley of words moving up the
steps and sliding back down. My father stares up at me, and I feel my
mother standing behind.*

*"Stop it. Stop it," I say. "Don't say that. Stop saying mean things." My
voice grows louder as something in me bubbles. Anger? Annoyance? Fear?*

*"Go back to your room, Patrice. You don't understand." My father
walks away, and the door to his basement office slams. Behind me my
mother disappears into their bedroom. I'm left on the middle step, where
I lean against the cold wall. By the time I stand up, I wear an imprint of
the wall's texture on my temple and the side of my forehead.*

*In the background the soundtrack continues with the levity of Top 40
hits.*

I've seen my share of dying malls. A few cars may sit near the
entrance while a scraggly tree or two sway in the wind. In the parking lot, dotted with potholes, pebbles skip across deserted concrete
that once held rows bursting with cars. A large sign hangs over the
entrance. "Yes, We're Still Open," the taut plastic reads. Inside an

elderly couple rummages through a clearance rack. A handful of workers stand behind the counters of the food court peddling soft pretzels and day-old cookies. The shops with the lights still on display unfamiliar names because the chain stores have vanished, leaving behind only local establishments.

Still alive. For now. Are dying marriages any different?

In the eighties, when I was growing up, the idea of divorce no longer shocked as it had previous generations. My childhood friends and classmates shuffled between parents every other weekend and through the summer. Still, my breath shortened into rapid pants when my parents separated after twenty-three years when I was eighteen.

What makes a marriage survive? A cup of love? A bushel of respect? The anchor of loyalty? Uncompromising fidelity? Extra laughter? A shared purpose? A common faith? Perhaps all of that? Perhaps more?

Holding my wedding pictures, I stare at my scarlet dress, which reminds me of the small, faded photograph on the wall of my childhood home. Framed inside, the twenty-something version of my father wears a bright red suit. His arm loops through the arm of my mother, who's dressed in a traditional white gown.

When Nyasha and I lace our fingers together and sit close, is there something our eyes ignore, hidden beneath what we create? A sign to illuminate what stretches beyond our view?

~⁀⁀

In the middle of the night, a few months after I marry Nyasha, my water glass accidentally crashes into shards against the tiles of our kitchen. In the dark I stand with my bare feet against the cold floor. Crumbs of glass splay around me, stretching beyond the beam of moonlight shining through the window. Not even a moment passes, and he stands at the light switch.

"Let me get your slippers," he says as he switches on the light.

"I'm sorry," I say. "So sorry." Fat tears appear in the corners of my eyes.

"Not to worry," he says, setting my slippers on the ground, reaching for me. "Why don't you go back to bed. I can take care of this."

Back in the room under the comforting weight of the duvet, I see the yellow light from the kitchen, hear the crinkle of swept glass, and wonder why I am still crying.

In the year following my parents' divorce, I asked my sister if she was surprised when she heard. Beneath my question there was a longing to share the remembrance of the unexpected.

"Not really. They used to fight," she said matter-of-factly.

A while back I returned to my hometown and walked through the University Center. I was surprised to see a building I thought dead still limping along. A year earlier the mall had seemed destined for dark hallways and caves of empty shops. "The local university gave it new life," my mother explained. "They reclaimed it as an extension of their campus."

My mother and I joined a sprinkling of other mall walkers in search of sanctuary from the single-digit temperatures beyond the sliding glass doors. We walked the faded hallways with their smattering of shops—a furniture store, a hair salon, a restaurant, all butting up against the green and yellow wing owned by the university. In the repurposed section I saw that the portrait studio had transformed into meeting rooms. The bookstore had become an office or a classroom. When I reached the entrance of the old movie theater, the lights were turned off. The locked door refused to let me see what now existed in the dark space.

As I touched the metal handle of the once familiar door, I felt transported back to my final time in the old theater, several months before my parents announced their divorce. In that awkward summer between high school graduation and the start of college, when my friends and I had shed girlhood but had yet to determine what womanhood looked like, we filled a row in one of the dark theaters. Tubs of warm popcorn and boxes of M&Ms moved up and down the line. In the smooth vinyl seats, I watched as Julia Roberts tried to sabotage her best friend's wedding. Along with everyone else, I walked out of the theater believing something magical about marriage.

I'm six or seven years old. In front of their bedroom mirror, my father's arms wrap around my mother's body. He leans over and kisses the top of her head and feels her silky hair beneath his lips. For a moment I watch and then burrow between them to stretch their hug to include me.

Despite the past, I still believe in lifetime marriages, with elderly couples and their wrinkled palms pressed together. On my wedding day I walked down the aisle sandwiched between my parents. I rested one arm on the curve of my father's elbow while I looped the other through my mother's arm. As our trio of bodies moved as a unit, I pretended that I walked between something breathing, something that still flourished. Moments later I stood before my husband. Our hands entwined and eyes alive, we made vows to begin. We slipped rings on our fingers, the cool metal sliding on clammy flesh. While my sister held my white calla lilies with the scarlet bow, my husband and I declared forever to each other. And with our fingers laced together, we walked back down the aisle into something new.

And I still give my subconscious space to imagine. In routine moments of life like a drive home, I let myself see my parents together. I envision my daughters speaking of Grandma and Grandpa as a single phrase. When my palm brushes my daughters' smooth cheeks, I pretend the place where I thought I would bring my children to swaddle them in the memories of my childhood still exists.

∼

I started running after my parents called during my first year of college to announce their divorce. I ran down the hallway to where everyone gathered in a friend's dorm room. Then I ran to the mall, where I swiped my credit card as if it were a magic wand that could give me a different life—ribbed turtlenecks, soft sweaters, double-zip boots. Perhaps beautiful clothes draping me could make my life beautiful, I thought.

Finally I sprinted across the world—a decade of traipsing the globe. I called it "finding myself" or "spreading my wings." I believed tired clichés could disguise my desire not to go home. A year in England. A visit to Kenya. A semester in Spain. A first job in upstate New York, where I knew no one. Christmases with my mother, but Thanksgivings spent with a college friend's family to avoid interacting with my father and his new wife.

During a backpacking trip across Europe, as a night train zipped from Rome to Venice, I refused to admit to a friend that I longed for a beautiful marriage that lasted. I looked out the window into the darkness and said that I didn't believe in love and certainly not the kind of love that could survive the years.

And then I met Nyasha. On the final stretch of my lap around the world, twenty minutes after my plane landed, I met this quiet man. He listened while I made sweeping statements about how I would make the world a better place. He challenged me to give greater thought to what I said. Our conversations hovered in the realm of ideas, and his reserved ways balanced my impulsive personality. At the end of the ten weeks, we stood in the international departures terminal of Cape Town's airport.

"I'll write," Nyasha said.

"Once a month?" I asked, attempting to make the moment light. I forced a teasing smile to appear on my face.

His face mirrored mine. "At least once a month. Absolute minimum." His arms wrapped around me and drew me close before his whispered response tickled my ear. "And maybe more."

Fifteen years after my parents divorced, they still don't communicate with each other, and I don't talk much with them about the past. My father speaks in hyperbole tainted with anger, a conversation combination I avoid. My mother's eyes grow sad. It's a clothing store of blame where everything that could have gone wrong fits the other person. But crumbs of the past trickle between their words, and I become a timid mouse trailing behind, grabbing phrases, sniffing them inside.

"Be careful. Some women don't care that your husband is married," my mother says as she helps me bring in the groceries.

"Don't try and change him," my father remarks while the ocean salts the air and our feet sink into sand near where Nyasha and I will wed.

"You remember Grandpa," Sekai says to my mother. My daughter stands in the doorway of the laundry room and holds the phone to her ear. From where I crouch pulling warm clothes from the drier, I can hear her side of the conversation unfold. My father and his wife left yesterday, and Sekai is telling my mother about their visit.

"Gammy, you remember Grandpa. When Mommy and Auntie were girls, you were together a mommy and a daddy."

For the length of my mother's response, I stop my work. Rather than remembering the past, I linger over the fresh smell of my husband's shirts and my daughter's pastel socks.

One day I may ask my parents what happened to their marriage. Maybe we'll sit across from each other in an all-night diner with thick slices of blueberry pie between us. As my fork scrapes the remains of the violet filling, I'll ask them if they understand what happened or how their marriage could have been different.

I imagine my father raising his Diet Coke with beads of condensation sliding down the glass and my mother squeezing a fresh lemon into her hot tea. From across the table they will look away from me for a moment. All around us waitresses will take orders, plates will hit tables, and perhaps a glass will break in the kitchen so the silence at our table won't become awkward. Then they'll begin to speak—slow at first, then gaining momentum.

Perhaps the talk will center on what disappeared, how they changed, or on what wasn't there from the beginning. Maybe I'll discover some answers. Or perhaps just sitting together will be more important than what I hear. As the night transforms to morning and the smell of scrambled eggs and bacon wafts past us, I will reach my hands across the table and rest mine in theirs. My cheeks damp, I'll tell them, "It's okay. We are okay."

~

A few weeks before Christmas, Nyasha, the girls, and I arrive at the side entrance of a mall. Not Eastland Mall, with its empty parking lot stretching wide, its wrecking balls and broken concrete, but another

184

mall in Charlotte where cars circle and circle in search of a spot near the door. The windowless structure beckons for people to disappear into its world of shiny trinkets and the smell of new clothes. With our outfits coordinated in red and faces ready to smile, we join other families in the portrait studio waiting our turn. Just as I straighten Sekai's dress and slide a matching headband on the baby, the photographer calls for us.

Christmas music bounces in the background, mixed with the rumble of waiting voices. "Move in. Your faces almost touching," the photographer says as she snaps an image. Then she stretches us into a row and, with the help of stools and boxes, staggers our heights into a descending staircase. Arms rest on shoulders, and I hold Shamiso in my lap.

In a week or so I will find a slim package with our family prints waiting on the stoop. Sekai will sit near me as I tug at the cardboard to release our memories. Later I will hold up the two eight-by-tens of our family for her to choose between. "Which one should we display?" I will say to her.

Sekai will stare first at the one of our faces almost pressed together and then at the one of our staggered heights. She will point to the second photo, the one where Nyasha and I sit in the middle, Sekai leans against her father, and I hold Shamiso in my lap. "We are all looking ahead in this one," she will say. As I slide the new family photo into the frame and place it on our bookshelf, I will think that she is right. We all look ahead, this small family—linked together, staring at what may come.

But today, after we sit for the portrait, we leave through the side entrance of a mall. I hold Sekai against my hip, and Nyasha carries the infant car seat. Beyond the doors thick raindrops plop against the ground, and the musty smell of wet cement tells me to inhale this moment and remember the day. We stand beneath the massive umbrella of awning that stretches over our heads for just a moment before Nyasha suggests I wait while he gets the car.

As he sets the baby next to me, his palm brushes against my bare skin. The touch of warmth against the chill creeping through my fingers reminds me of the beauty of all that remains. I watch my husband walk across the parking lot, through the rain, and I think this moment could be hallowed ground.

Chapter 24

Marching Toward Zion

On a Sunday in mid-December, as on most other Sundays, I return home from church tired, ready to eat a few bites of food before succumbing to rest. My eyes droop from the weight of desired sleep, and I think of my bed and the fleece blanket I love to pull to my chin.

"Go lie down," Nyasha says to me, taking my lunch plate and carrying it to the sink. "Go lie down." I let his words push me toward the stairs. For perhaps an hour or maybe more, my body and my mind sink into soft places. A deep sleep takes over and sends me tumbling and falling into a world of dreams and impossible things.

I wonder if I nap more this winter than I have in the past. If there is a certain weariness I can't shake no matter how often I close my eyes. Is my body giving in to a desire to escape that I can't recognize while awake? Perhaps these Sunday afternoon naps cross too far into evening. Maybe I do wake still carrying the weight of exhaustion. As the daylight dims, I stare beyond my bedroom window past the bare branches of my neighbor's tree, and I watch a world drained of color carrying on in washed-out grays. Then I let the comfort of the bed tug me back to sleep.

My family and I have been attending a predominantly white church in Charlotte for almost two years now. As a black family, we are in the minority in our congregation, just as we are in our country.

In the United States nearly nine out of ten churches are considered segregated, with 80 percent or more of the membership coming from one racial group. Almost sixty years ago Dr. Martin Luther King Jr. declared Sunday mornings to be "the most segregated hour of Christian America."[1] The reality, though, in modern America, is that many congregations aren't segregated because of some form of racial animosity. Something much simpler manifests itself across the country on Sunday mornings: people tend to feel more comfortable with people who look like themselves. And people who have similar styles of worship often have similar colors of skin.

Nyasha and I didn't choose to start attending our church out of a belief in the integration of Sunday mornings. We came because I saw light in the sanctuary. Bright light shone through the large windows. Golden rays pierced the gray cloud that followed me wherever I stepped. Lyrics to a song appeared on the large screen as we walked in, and I wanted to sit on the hard pew and feel the smooth wood slick under my palm. I reached for Nyasha, and my body stilled while first one tear and then another rolled down my cheek.

The previous few years marked one of those difficult seasons of life that everyone has experienced or will experience. In the midst of it all, Nyasha and I spent Sunday mornings searching for a church that might help us cling to our faith. With our shared history in multicultural congregations, I was surprised we visited a white church and eventually wanted to stay. We smiled at the white faces filling the sanctuary and pressed our brown hands into the pink hands of others. Something washed over us. Calm? Peace? Healing? Whatever that thing was nudged the rain cloud overhead and let the warm light from the great windows soothe at least some of our wounds.

This winter, though, our second in this church, I think more and more about our black family in a mostly white congregation. The apostle Paul wrote that in the Christian faith "there is neither Jew nor Gentile."[2] Yet sometimes I think how black and white still remain. When we first visited our church, we chose to ignore what we knew we couldn't ignore forever. But after the gray cloud started to fade, moments of discomfort found me when I scanned the crowd, searching for a face like mine. I reminded myself that race forms just a piece of a person's identity. Still I didn't mind the times we left through the side doors as soon as the service ended.

As the months passed, I began to notice how I parsed my sentences with greater caution, nervous that I might offend—or, worse, be labeled the black woman who can't get past the tired topic of race. Rather than explaining how white views of beauty impose their standards on black hair textures, I overlooked a comment about "good" hair. Somewhere in my logic I declared "pleasant" more important than "truthful."

Just before the Christmas break, I receive a phone call from five-year-old Sekai's school. Her temperature is well above normal. Leaving the breakfast dishes in the sink, I bundle up my toddler, Shamiso, and go to pick up my sick girl. By the time I carry Sekai to her bed, her temperature has spiked to a solid 103 degrees. I draw her blinds, tuck the covers around her, and let my lips touch her warm forehead. *The body needs rest and fluids*, I think. *Rest.*

As illness moves through our home, we miss the last Sunday before Christmas, when the church lights the final Advent candle. A few days later, with both Shamiso and Nyasha now sick, we also miss the Christmas Eve service. That night with a sick child in my arms, I think of what it might have been for our voices to join the sweet voices of others in "Silent Night." In my imagination I see the congregation clutch candles, touch the wicks together, and pass the bright flame down each row.

Instead of wisps of fire in a dim room, during this year's darkest days, I instruct my family to rest. Drink fluids. And rest some more. When I think of the sanctuary dotted with yellow light and the beauty of "Silent Night" calming the evening, I search for disappointment woven in with the aroma of chicken soup. I think a bit of sadness might turn the taste of honey tea bitter. But the soup smells like stock and thyme. The tea tastes sweet as it soothes sore throats. And in our house I feel a great stillness.

$\sim$

In early January I sit in my parked car in front of Shamiso's preschool. With the phone near my ear, I chat for a few minutes with my friend Joy. We use these short moments just after preschool drop-off or just before pick-up to connect with each other. Around me I see the cars of other parents pull into spots, and a few children emerge through the school doors. Our time is short, and we rush our conversation, knowing the rest of the day brings few gaps.

Joy befriended me at church shortly after my family and I arrived. Besides her invitation to join a writing group, her two girls and my two girls are close in age. And between discussions about parenting and faith, Joy speaks with me about race. She is one of the few white women I know who verbalizes the importance of understanding racial injustice.

I feel safer revealing more of my thoughts to her than I would with the average white person because she admits to limitations in her awareness and approaches our conversations with humility. With Joy I stumble through my opinion about police killings of unarmed black men or I touch on society's color hierarchy present in beauty standards. As our children shriek around us, our conversations can brush against awkward.

"Don't you think sometimes people have more in common with someone of another race than they do with people who look like them?" Joy asked me one afternoon after a lunch of grilled-cheese sandwiches. Our girls ran around my kitchen island. I paused to smile at their antics, clean up a few toys, and think how to respond to Joy's statement in a way that affirmed her observation but also wove in flecks of a nuanced truth.

"I think it's true that race is just a part of a person, and because of that people can connect on so many different points," I said as I tossed blocks into their mesh bag. "But I still think that sometimes only a person who looks like me can understand certain things about me. Like what it feels like to walk into a room and consistently be the only person of my race."

From where she sat on the floor leaning back against the couch, she looked at me and nodded. My mouth curled in a slight smile of gratitude.

With friends like Joy, I worry less about saying too many things that might make a white person uncomfortable. I don't necessarily flee from the topic of race. However, I know these conversations often become a diluted version of what I might say with my black friends.

"Are you going to the church night out on Friday?" Joy asks me in the last minute or two before I need to get Shamiso from her class. Our church is one of those places where participation can extend beyond the hour-and-a-half Sunday morning service. Monthly lunches, mid-week meetings, social gatherings, small groups. Nyasha and I tend to skip many of these activities.

"Maybe," I say. I think of Sekai's ballet practice on Friday evening. It's only Tuesday, but I know that by Friday Nyasha will be ready to rest. These reasons seem to lack heft. While Nyasha and I sometimes find these events tiring because we feel on the fringe of our church, I don't say that to Joy.

In this church culture I know the only way to stop feeling like an outsider is to participate, to go to events, to meet people. But I remember the previous weekend at an introductory meeting for a small group. Dessert and drinks. People mingling and swapping small-talk stories. Nyasha and I were the only nonwhite people in the room.

But other people have things that make them different too, I told myself as I sipped on a glass of red wine. Perhaps. But from my view, those differences didn't reveal themselves with a mere glance at another person. As we grouped together in a circle, I noticed myself disappearing—the talkative Patrice, the Patrice quick to smile and laugh. In her place the soft-voiced and hesitant version of myself inhabited my body for the rest of the evening. My normal personality returned after Nyasha and I said our goodbyes and drove away in our car.

"Yeah, no," I say to Joy with greater certainty. "We probably won't be there."

There are only so many times in a week or a month that I might choose to be in such a drastic minority, and this week I already feel weary of the idea. I know Nyasha and I will spend Friday evening at home. After we move through the rituals of eating dinner, bathing the girls, and putting them to bed, we will sit on the couch with my legs resting across his lap. As we drink warm mugs of tea, I will hear our voices decompress the week behind us. Our talk will meander through the stories that make us smile and the ones that make us shake our fists. As the conversation fades into evening, I may doze off feeling the comfort of my husband's presence nearby.

On another evening in mid-January, Nyasha and I are talking about church, and I ask, "Is this working?" The lights in our room are out, and the glow of the streetlight seeps through the closed blinds. Beyond the windows I hear the rumble of a driving car, and I wonder at the shape of the moon—perhaps just a sliver tonight.

This conversation isn't new. It creeps in while Nyasha washes the dishes or I pack lunches for the girls. It hides behind the banality of grocery lists and dental appointments. It shows itself in the quietest moments of wakefulness.

"In the beginning I felt more connected than I do today," he says. "And I think it's my fault. I'm not trying hard enough." He turns his head toward me, and I rest mine on his shoulder.

Months back, when we decided to join our church, I remember a man at our membership class saying how friendly and welcoming our church was—which I agreed with then and still agree with now. He then said, "If people aren't connecting here, it's because they aren't trying." Even though I thought of the couple of lovely friendships I had already formed, I flinched at his words. *Trying.* My shoulders sagged a bit from the burden thrust on me.

Try harder, I thought. *Try harder.* I glanced at the owner of the voice. A white man. *He fits here,* I thought. *At least he fits here better than me.*

I hear Nyasha's words now. And it occurs to me that these days I am not trying to belong. Maybe I once was. But this winter I am guilty of not trying. Because doesn't trying to belong involve a greater outpouring of effort? Showing up at events? Staying to chat? Working to smooth the sharp edges and stick a square peg through a round hole?

"Remember a few weeks ago at the small group gathering?" I ask Nyasha. He nods, and I know we both think the same thing. How we climbed into our car, looked at each other, and I said, "I think we want a community but not necessarily one where everyone looks the same except us." When Nyasha stopped the car at a light, he turned to me and smiled. "I was thinking the same thing."

Studies indicate that my family's tenure at our church will be less than a white person's stay. Minority groups tend to feel on the fringe, like outsiders, says the research. They don't feel like they belong. Not just black people in white churches, but any minority group in a church with an overwhelming majority.[3]

But Nyasha and I are people and not data points. And now in this place we call our church home, I wonder if maybe I want to remain on the fringe. Perhaps I am scared of what will happen when too many friendships develop where pieces of me lie dormant. Maybe somewhere in me I believe that this dominant culture will allow only some parts of me to rise up and speak and exist. And before I realize what shifts around me, I will interact with people of mostly one color, I will attend events populated by shades of peach skin. Perhaps it's easier if I linger at the edge, form just a few good friendships, and remain content with not too much more.

Could it be that I'm not trying to belong because I want to remain my true self?

But what of the light that first poured over me, a golden balm of healing in each ray? I think of the meals strangers showered over us after Shamiso's birth. The way we still occupy the back row week after week and no one pushes us further than we want. At some point this question of belonging had to surface, this reality of choosing to be one of a few black people in a large crowd. Perhaps the question—at least for now—is not if this is working, but rather how can we make this place we have chosen work? How can we keep from becoming worn?

Nyasha and I don't ponder the conversation more. Our talk slows, and our words drift toward a sea of dreams.

The week before the country celebrates the legacy of Dr. Martin Luther King Jr., Nyasha has a random vacation day. With the girls in school, we decide to watch *Selma*. We join a handful of other movie patrons for the first show of the day. Maybe eight of us cluster near the ticket counter. Nyasha's and my skin blends into everyone else's varied shades of brown, including that of the movie theater employee. We all give money and credit cards as the man behind the counter distributes tickets printed on thin paper. In the air the scent of fresh popcorn coated in liquid butter tempts me for a moment before I remember it never tastes as good as it smells.

"Which seats do you want?" the man asks. The small screen in front of us displays all the seats in the theater.

"The middle," Nyasha answers.

"*Selma*," I say. "Did we tell you that we're here to see *Selma*?"

The man stops, looks at us, glances at the other people, and then says, "Well, I just assumed you were here for that. It's the first show of the day."

I smile. "We are. I just wanted to make sure. I wasn't sure if we had said it."

A man behind us in line laughs. "Aren't we all here for the same thing?"

Yes, we're here for the same thing, I think. *We are all here for the same thing.* When Nyasha and I settle into our seats a few minutes later, the small group of people we stood in line with scatters throughout the empty rows. Some sit a bit behind us. One couple sits to our left. A few others sit in front of us. Nyasha is the only person sitting next to me, but I feel as if the empty seats disappear. For two hours we watch Dr. King and many others march for voting rights in Selma, Alabama. When the movie ends, for the length of the closing credits, we all remain still.

Later, back at home, I sit on my bed. But I'm not tired today. I remain awake and turn toward the window, staring past the staggered shingles of our roof to our neighbor's tree, its tentacles of bare branches reaching for the sun. In its dormant state, absent bright, green leaves or the rustle of birds nesting in limbs, the tree still stands proud and tall.

It's Martin Luther King Jr. Day, and beyond the doors of the Gantt Center for African-American Arts + Culture, life in uptown Charlotte carries on. Companies operate, and men and women in business attire walk through revolving doors after lunch breaks. But here on the second floor of the cultural center, Sekai and I sit in front-row seats with Shamiso in my lap. Before us a woman with beautiful locks stands and speaks with thunder into the microphone. She wears a white dress, a contrast against her deep-brown skin. Streaming in from the floor-to-ceiling windows behind her, golden light shines.

We are here to sing freedom songs, bold music that once flooded the air in pursuit of change. "In remembrance of those who fought for freedom," the woman says. Men and women, children and elders, those in seats and the crowd standing around—we lift our voices in unison. We sing of letting our little light shine.

As I feel my daughters near me and see us as part of this crowd, I think our earthly voices dance with the voices of angels, a small accompaniment to a profound beauty. In the midst of these strangers, I look around at skin colors across a great spectrum of brown. With the calming melody in my ear, I can see this gathering of people for what it is—a space where questions fade, explanations cease, and discomfort falls away. Freedom songs spread through the air once again, flaming wicks that pass from streets to bridges, from towns to cities with cries for civil rights and sweet harmony.

Chapter 25

For My Husband Driving Down a Mountain

After Philando Castile's death in St. Paul and Alton Sterling's in Baton Rouge, after too many men gone with skin the shade of yours—after all this, I waved goodbye. A week we'd spent here in the cool of these mountains, and the plans already in place for just me to remain. So I stood amid the perfume of sweet air and sharp evergreens, stood with my hand raised while you journeyed away. "Next week," I called after you. "I'll see you when you return next week." One hundred thirty miles between this mountain and our home.

Earlier that morning, after we wandered the short stretch of a small town's main road, after we popped into a furniture store that smelled of stained pine, after—yes, after—I spotted a row of black Sambo dolls perched on a dusty shelf—an image I wanted this world to burn long ago—after all this, I pulled open the door to an art gallery and heard a bell chime. The shop owner, with her silver hair and firm wrinkles etched into her pale face, ushered us through the entryway. Our senses took in the white walls, the cream shelves filled with orange and red glass, the scent of canvas and pottery, ink and paint.

"You must be newlyweds," she said. You and I, we glanced at each other. You touched my arm, and your lips parted into that familiar grin.

"Almost eight years," I replied.

"So young, so young," and I think she wanted to reach her weathered hands for ours, but instead she gave us a tour of the art in that brightly lit place. When she found out that I am a writer, she tilted her head to the side. "So much to write about now." Her words dissipated into a sigh, but I still heard all that she didn't say.

The headlines say our country is in crisis, and I think about all that smolders and the temperatures that rise with the weariness of these recent days. She muttered, "Good people know good people, and that's all that matters." She blew us a kiss as we walked away, arm in arm, a breath of air that might ignite a spark or extinguish a flame.

After Philando Castile's death in St. Paul and Alton Sterling's in Baton Rouge, after your car pulled away, I called out, "Goodbye," to you. I can't remember if I took my palm to my lips and gifted you a kiss across the empty space, but I tell myself that you caught all that I wanted to say. *Please, my love, keep your hands on the wheel, your registration close. Keep your speed under the limit and go straight home.*

I watched your car's dusty bumper shrinking out of sight, the start of your spiral down that mountain, your return to the heat of our burning unknown. All I could do was reach out my open hand and wave.

Chapter 26

An Abundance of
Impossible Things

In the spring prior to the Charleston church massacre, during my daily commute to my older daughter's school, I noticed a wad of faded red fabric drooping from a flagpole outside of a stranger's house.

It couldn't be.

I pulled right to slow down in my lane and looked once and then again to verify. There, tucked beneath the folds of the familiar stars and stripes, two blue lines crossed over the red fabric with the telltale white stars.

Was this new? How had I never noticed?

Like many other transplants to Charlotte, I like to think the Confederate flag exists in other parts of the South but not in this modern city that boasts tall buildings and black mayors. The New South. A city that embraces diversity and has rid itself of its racist past.

Yet there it was. Tattered, weathered. Just like the American flag that hung above it. *First country and then the South*, I thought as I glanced at the rest of the yard.

What if, rather than driving by, I were walking on the sidewalk in front of this house, pushing my toddler in her stroller? What if the owners were sitting on their front porch as I passed? Would they stare at my brown skin and scowl? Would their faces express scorn at my presence on the sidewalk, hoping I would leave because they believed my blackness could dirty their property? Or maybe they would offer me a smile, a wave, a sign of welcome even as their flag signaled other sentiments.

Later that evening, at my Wednesday night Bible study, I decided to mention the flag to the women in my group. A thin wall divided our small room from the sanctuary, where musicians practiced for the Sunday service. The sounds of a keyboard, guitars, and drums provided background music as we talked. Muffled voices sang of strivings that ceased and a hope not rooted in earthly things. I looked around at the white faces of my group and wanted to retreat from my questions, to hum along with songs I had sung many times before, to forget the Confederate flag I had seen that day.

"What are people trying to say with the flag?" I asked. "What do they want to communicate?" Two women with long histories living in the South glanced at each other. One opened her mouth with the beginning of a response.

At that moment a visitor walked through the door, and conversation shifted to greetings for the newcomer. Introductions and personal stories were accompanied by a murmur of lyrics pleading for an end to troubles. I spoke words of welcome and asked the new woman appropriate questions about herself, her family, her background. Beyond the wall one song transitioned to the next while we settled into our seats for the evening. The Confederate flag remained in my thoughts, but I couldn't find a way to return to the topic. Later that night I drove past the flag hanging in the soft spring twilight and returned to my home without answers.

Just weeks after the massacre, while visiting my mother's home in Anchorage, I sorted through piles of stuff from my college and graduate school years. I tossed an old copy of *Black Enterprise* to Nyasha.

"This is how we got to Charlotte," I said.

He caught the magazine and looked at the glossy cover, which featured a smiling black family with a sparkling city skyline in the backdrop. A bold headline read, "Top 10 Cities for African Americans." He looked up at me and laughed.

When we were leaving Cape Town and choosing somewhere to live, I'd remembered that article from years ago. Charlotte seemed like a place filled with possibility for our black family, a city exploding with a bounty of opportunities.

"Who could've guessed this would define our future," he said, handing the magazine back to me. I held it for a moment, wondering if I should save this memento along with the other scraps I had collected of my life in Anchorage. I stared at the image of the happy family for another minute before putting the magazine in the pile of papers to recycle.

Back in early spring, when we booked our July tickets to Anchorage, all I could envision was how desperately hot and unbearable Charlotte becomes each summer. But then in mid-June a white man walked into a black church in Charleston, South Carolina, and killed Reverend Clementa Pinckney, Cynthia Hurd, Reverend Sharonda Coleman-Singleton, Tywanza Sanders, Ethel Lance, Susie Jackson, Reverend Depayne Middleton-Doctor, Reverend Daniel Simmons, and Myra Thompson.[1]

The near hundred-degree-days in the South began to boil with words and tension and accusation. And, in my case, fear. I tried to forget that the shooter had stopped at a gas station in Charlotte after he fled Charleston.[2] And as the country debated the use and place of the Confederate flag, I kept hoping the flag I had first spotted that spring day, sagging against a stranger's flagpole, might disappear.

I searched for it every time I passed the gas station and then the grocery store where I often stopped to grab a bag of apples or a final ingredient for dinner. As it hung below the American flag, I could always see the blue bars and red background almost blocked by the green branches of a tree.

After the massacre, instead of feeling a sense of repulsion at the sight of the flag or a need to turn my gaze, I found myself pausing to confirm the flag's presence. I made a point to glance at the muted colors hanging limp against the pole, with never enough breeze to send the fabric flapping in the wind.

And I welcomed our trip to my Alaskan home in a way I couldn't have predicted back in March. "I want to leave," I told Nyasha late one night as I sorted clothes and filled suitcases. "I don't want to be here." I longed to take my family and exist somewhere else, thousands of miles away. I dreamed of a place where the summer days were chilly enough that one's breath danced in the morning.

In early July, a week after my family and I arrived in Anchorage, we drove under overcast skies to Portage Glacier. Our car threaded around bends and curves of the Seward Highway, and beyond the windows sharp cliffs rose on our left, and the silt of Cook Inlet flanked our right. During the drive, I thought of my childhood trips to Portage Glacier and other parts of the Kenai Peninsula and how on many days the sun would glisten off the water. Even though years had passed since I'd last driven this road, my hands could anticipate the next bend. My foot knew when to sink against the brake, when to tap the gas.

In the background of our car conversation, the radio played intermittent news that moved between crackle and clear. South Carolina had voted to remove the Confederate flag from the statehouse grounds, a reporter said, to lower it with respect and move the old symbol to the nearby military museum. From the backseat, five-year-old Sekai stared out the window at the mud flats and the inlet, and I wondered if the words meant anything to her. Perhaps she dreamed only of wide open spaces and time with her parents.

On-and-off rain showers glazed the road and draped over the mountains just across the water. A cozy feeling settled over me, an almost perfect feeling. Our little family protected from the rain falling beyond our window, hearing how parts of our country now recognized that perhaps the Confederate flag belonged with the past.

"It's crazy it took what happened in Charleston . . ." My voice trailed off, the rest implied. Nyasha nodded at me. Later we listened to a professor from a college in South Carolina explain how many white people were *unaware* that the flag offended others in this way. "Now they've come to realize," he added. I imagined he thought the explanations birthed some form of absolution.

I wanted to believe the professor, to believe it possible that people hadn't known. This symbol reminded me of the sad history of my country and told me what I would have been had I lived two hundred years ago. I wanted to imagine that the family flying the flag back in Charlotte didn't wish to live in the past. I wanted to believe that the person driving a truck with the Confederate flag stuck to the bumper didn't want to return to a time when people like me, my husband, and my girls were property. An era when, at thirty-five years old, I would have already outlived the life expectancy of a black woman held in slavery.[3]

I suspect, though, that these people just cared about their state and region. Perhaps they'd grown weary of others in the country treating them as if they should live in embarrassment and shame. As they sought to create a sense of respect for themselves and the place they called home, they didn't realize that those colors, that pattern offended others. Scared me.

Years ago at my church in Anchorage, a young man had stood on the stage with several other high school seniors receiving gifts, certificates, and prayers for graduation and what was to come. Those around me surely laughed and celebrated that morning, but I remember only the Confederate flag screen-printed across the young man's denim shirt, tucked into a pair of jeans with a shiny buckle with the same symbol. I remember looking around at the many white faces that surrounded me on all sides. Did they see what I saw? Did they notice the diagonal bars?

The young man's hair was brown—I remember that too. But that's all. I recall nothing of what he told the church about his future plans when the youth pastor pushed the microphone in front of his face. Nothing about his parents or whether I had ever met them. All that remains is the memory of the belt buckle and a young man cloaked in a Confederate flag. I stared at him, unable to avert my eyes. *He doesn't know, he just doesn't know,* I told myself that morning as he stood among a group of young people almost elevated off the ground by the power of their dreams.

"We were unaware," the professor had said. "We were unaware." Now we're aware.

A few days after the Portage Glacier outing, Nyasha and I slipped from my mother's home just past ten o'clock into an evening as bright as the day. With the girls put to bed, the parents got to revel in a sun that still hung high in the sky. We wandered through the different roads of my mother's neighborhood, and I told Nyasha how I longed for Anchorage, how sometimes I wondered if we should leave Charlotte and make this city our home.

"It won't be like it used to be," Nyasha said as we wove around the cul-de-sac behind my mother's house. We passed a house I knew would go on the market soon. A few days earlier, while walking this same route alone, I had stopped and talked to a man cutting wood in his garage. "I'm doing a few repairs to the place before I try to sell it," he told me. He now lived in Texas, and it was time to break his ties to Alaska.

I didn't mention the impending For Sale sign to Nyasha. We kept walking along the circle of houses and back onto the busier road.

"And you know there's the winter too," he added.

Nyasha wasn't trying to discourage me. One of the things I love about him is his willingness to embrace my schemes. Still, from time to time, his words infuse practicality into my pipe dreams.

"Yes, I know," I said, stepping around a puddle. I thought of the ice and snow, the way these endless summer days would diminish into long winter nights. Still, I kept thinking of the house that would soon sit with a For Sale sign in its front yard.

As Nyasha and I neared my mother's home, I pointed to a house down the block from hers. You could see the house from her front bedroom if you stood at the window and pressed your right cheek against the glass.

"That house used to have a Confederate flag hanging in its garage," I said. I'd lived with my mother the year before Nyasha and I married, and nearly every morning I had crept from my mother's home and walked through this neighborhood and past that house. Occasionally the garage door had been left open, and the familiar colors and pattern and bold stars covered a chunk of the wall on the right side.

I never saw the people who lived there, so I used to create their story in my mind. People from the South, proud of their roots. People much like the young man who stood at the front of the church that Sunday, somehow oblivious to the possibility that this flag might upset others. I used to mention the flag to my mother, but she'd never seen the garage open. Today, as usual, the garage door was closed.

The evening sunlight transformed to threads of color, beginning the transition to dusk. We crossed the street and walked up the path to my mother's front step, the overgrown ferns along the way batting at my legs. I turned back to glance at the closed garage. Perhaps the flag vanished long ago. Maybe new neighbors lived in this home, and their garage wall held hooks stocked with rakes and snow shovels.

"It won't be like it used to be," Nyasha had said, and I wanted to believe that sometimes life could be even better.

~ᴗ

In mid-July we returned to Charlotte. Little seemed to have changed. The fierce heat still held the city captive. In June we had left behind a patch of dry grass in the backyard, and we returned to yellow spreading through the green. Just past the gas station and grocery store, the faded Confederate flag still twisted around the pole beneath the American flag. Within a few days back in the heat, I forgot what it was like to visit a park in midday or smell the scent of crisp air after an early-evening drizzle. Inside, I inhaled the stale recycled odor of our air-conditioned house.

Not long after we returned to Charlotte, the children's director at our church asked Nyasha and me if we could help in Shamiso's class that coming Sunday. Even as I agreed, I cringed. I wanted our family together. I didn't want Nyasha, Shamiso, and me in the toddler room while Sekai learned Bible verses and sang about Jesus' love downstairs in the class for older children. And I couldn't understand my hesitation, the tightening I felt in my chest when I thought of our family separated on Sunday. We had always been apart on Sundays—Nyasha and me in the sanctuary, Shamiso with the other toddlers, and Sekai with her peers. When our pastor dismissed the congregation at the end of the service, we wound our way through the crowd and collected our children from their classrooms.

It had never bothered me to have our family separated. But that was before.

For days I'd been imagining someone walking into our church in search of black people. The faceless person would wander through the basement by the elementary-school rooms and hear giggles and laughs. He would lift his arm and aim his gun at children with brown skin.

In those hypnotic moments when my subconscious carved into the monotony of activity, when I was driving familiar streets or wiping down my kitchen counters, my mind warned of what might happen. I saw Sekai without her mother or father to shield her from harm, to protect her with our own bodies. I shuddered thinking of her without us, exposed, alone.

On the drive to church that Sunday, I saw the faded flag just as I had seen it in the weeks and months past. It stared at me as if it were a living thing that might fly away from the flagpole and spread its pattern and color and meaning across the land. I wanted to tell Nyasha to turn the car around, to return us to the refuge of our home, the place where we were safe behind our doors.

Despite so many calling for a lowering of the flag, these strangers kept theirs elevated. *They don't care*, I thought while my stomach churned with fears of church and separating our family and my little girl alone. If these people didn't care, how many more were like them?

"Mommy," Sekai said from the backseat, her words penetrating my thoughts. "Mommy, can I help you and Daddy in Shami's class? Can I come too?" Her words soothed me, called me back from whatever murky place my mind wanted to take me. Her questions summoned me out of my morbid fantasy and into the world as it is.

"Yes, baby. Yes, I think that would be fine." The car continued to move. Nyasha held the steering wheel. The girls laughed in the backseat. And I pretended that I hadn't just spent days envisioning a thing I longed to forget.

After a dry summer transformed our lawn to a mosaic of scraggly green and tan blades, the cusp of autumn brought not rain, but phantom thunder, rattling the air around me. Far-off, distant noises. Elsewhere in Charlotte, though not in my neighborhood, thick drops pounded against rooftops and flooded suburban streets. The air was damp, so damp I thought I could touch it, and I anticipated droplets of tears hiding in the humidity, an overflow about to pour.

Around the time the air grew moist, I noticed the house with the Confederate flag had replaced the old, tattered one with a crisp new one. Running along the top and bottom edge were a series of words I could never quite read.

I didn't ask anyone about the flag or its white lettering. Long gone from the news or heated discussion was the massacre at the church in Charleston. The world kept pushing forward, going back to school, discussing other tragedies across the globe. And the sky thundered. Nearly every time I stood on the sidewalk or drove down my street, I saw a bolt of lightning shoot to the ground.

Then one day the rains found us, buried our home and street in an endless staccato, the squeezing of moisture from the atmosphere.

Safe and dry inside, I thought of how the clouds can't keep the water forever. How nothing can hold back the inevitable.

"I don't think the grass will turn green again," I told Nyasha days later, after one storm and then another and another. Despite the velvet black-brown of damp earth, the grass refused to change.

Nyasha glanced out the sliding glass door. "I think it's done for the season. I don't think it's going to get better." The air cracked around me, signaling a coming storm, but I no longer hoped for green. I was already facing autumn, looking forward to winter.

A few weeks later I slid my feet under the blanket spread across my bed and disappeared into a book. Beyond the walls of the house, the wind billowed with great howls, and the rhythmic lullaby of rain pounding the roof and pavement below made me want to spin into a deep rest.

That autumn the humid air sweated great drops almost every day. Each morning held the tangy scent of wet concrete, a smell that to my delight never seemed to vanish. The rain gave me that held-in feeling I longed for, the cozy sensation of being wrapped in warmth, protected from the uncertain world beyond our door.

By the bookshelf, next to the opposite side of the bed, Nyasha stretched out stomach down on the floor, his elbows propped up by a pillow. "If you could live anywhere, where would you live?" His question broke through my reading trance and the steady beats of rain. "Anywhere. If you could live anywhere?"

The many drops continued to strike the ground, and the cadence of the storm helped me think. There was Anchorage, where I had grown up with the bounty of old friends and snow-covered peaks. But what then of the many places I had lived since leaving my hometown? Or the fullness of our lives in Charlotte? The church we attended, the school where Sekai sat behind a desk and smiled at teachers we loved, the way I could run an errand and see a friend choosing perfect toma-toes in the produce section.

Still, my mind wandered away from this city when I remembered my long-ago dream of the life I had envisioned when I'd first clutched that glossy magazine. The cover photo of the smiling black family. The gleaming cityscape rising behind them in the distance. Perhaps the open arms of opportunity and the promise of possibility weren't as real as I'd once believed. But were those desires even feasible in the imaginary life I sometimes created when I considered other places, other cities, other homes? Maybe those aches were artifacts of a naïve notion about what life could offer.

"I don't know," I said to Nyasha after several moments elapsed. "I don't know." If I wasn't sure I wanted to be in Charlotte, I should have had an answer. But I didn't know where I thought might be better.

"I thought you would say Anchorage," Nyasha said. I turned to meet his eyes, and he repeated, "I was sure you would say Alaska."

I'd thought I might have too. This decade of our thirties was like roses, fragrant and beautiful. Full, vibrant colors that Nyasha brought home. He would hold green stems gathered in his closed fist and tell me with a tender smile how much he loved me. Our lives felt solid. Our marriage. The soft faces of our daughters.

Yet this decade felt full of longing too. That night or another night, I might wake as something drew me from my bed. In the predawn hours, I would sit in the silver darkness with my thoughts. Another morning I would listen to Nyasha tell me of his sleepless night. He would tell how he spent the early hours wondering if we would ever feel rooted in this community—or any community. Maybe we were hoping to live a life that existed beyond the reality of our world.

That night he had asked me where I wanted to live. Other eve-nings we talked of all that was good and beautiful, yet those moments sometimes felt as fragile as the wings of a moth.

If you could live anywhere.

With Nyasha's question I wondered if again one thought could spiral to the next, and we would ask ourselves if we should start over, try again, pick a different place to believe in the magic of possibility, of opportunity. We watched day move to darkness, and I thought of roses and longing and the way the fragrant scent of petals can't hide sharp thorns.

"My mother told me earlier this week," I said to Nyasha, "that the winter chill is already in the air. I don't think we can do the Anchorage winters."

He nodded. I thought not so much in agreement but maybe in acknowledgement of things that were and the things we couldn't change.

Later that autumn I discovered the secret passage at the edge of my neighborhood. A new section of pavement connected the back of my community to the back of another community. One morning, in the brisk autumn temperatures, I ventured around the fluorescent orange cones and across the fresh asphalt, still a rich black from lack of wear. I dipped under a yellow, plastic streamer that prohibited cars from passing, but not mothers with strollers, I reasoned.

Shamiso and I shed the familiarity of our neighborhood, with houses pushed close together and a single tree in each front yard. We crossed over the new bridge that stretched above a small valley, dividing my neighborhood from another, splitting new and old. And I was transported to another world. My own Narnia, I thought as I walked beneath towering trees arching toward the sky, so tall that sunlight mixed with great shadows and the air chilled my exposed arms.

I pushed the stroller along the slim road and gazed at older homes that reminded me of a long- ago Charlotte I never knew. Great yards spread between the houses, enough space that a person couldn't tell whether or not a neighbor was home. A lazy stream crossed beneath the road, and above us the sky was almost clear but for the occasional puff of clouds.

I stopped and breathed in the smell of a mature forest, the rich, spicy flavor. Shamiso's face turned up toward the treetops high above. Her finger pointed to a lone bird gliding across the blue. For a moment I traveled back in time to my childhood neighborhood—the roads I biked down, the musky woods I played in, the soft moss I ran my fingers over, the bits of stagnant water I filled with pinecones and pebbles.

Here behind my Charlotte neighborhood, this place had existed all along. Just on the other side of a slight valley, beyond a gate of trees, right here was this bit of heaven.

I wanted to stay here, pushing Shamiso in her stroller. I wanted to remain on the other side of the bridge beyond the leafy gate. So we turned down a side road where tall trees curved into a canopy. The road narrowed, and the branches overhead kept the ribbon of pavement in complete shade.

Then, at the edge of someone's yard, I saw it. There in the dim, in this place that made me think of heaven, my eyes adjusted to the red, the blue diagonal lines, the stars of a Confederate flag.

My limbs trembled. Did I detect slight movement in the woods? The snap of a broken twig? Hidden in the shadows, who saw me standing here with my toddler in the stroller? A person who would voice a harsh word or an arm that would motion me away from this road?

But all that emerged was a sleek cat walking across the yard. Still I backed away, the flag growing smaller until I arrived at the larger road. There I turned and retraced my footsteps to the edge of those great trees, to the bridge that would return my child and me to my neighborhood, to the earth I knew.

A few weeks before Thanksgiving, Nyasha, the girls, and I pulled on coordinated vests. Nyasha spread a duvet cover over a patch of lawn in our backyard, and I gathered my family for our biannual picture. Since Sekai's birth, every two years we had set the timer of the camera and positioned our bodies with our stomachs flattened to the ground, our faces raised in smiles.

The first one was taken in Kirstenbosch, Cape Town's famous botanical garden, the second in the backyard of the house we lived in our first year in Charlotte. Two years ago, just after Shamiso's birth, we had spread a blanket across the front porch of an old farmhouse where some friends lived. Visitors to our home often noticed the progression of pictures scattered across the wall and commented about how our family had grown in age and size.

That afternoon in the waning daylight, I set the timer on my phone and squeezed myself on the flimsy duvet cover between Sekai and Nyasha. The burnt orange leaves splattered across the brilliant green.

"Three. Two. One," Sekai counted down.

"Smile, Shami," Nyasha said to our toddler through the grin on his face.

At the last moment I slid one arm through the bend of Nyasha's arm and laid the other over Sekai's back as Nyasha spread his other arm over Shamiso's. Our bodies had been close before, but with the warmth of limbs entwined, flesh next to flesh, there was a sense of linkage.

When I climbed from my spot to set the timer again, I commented to Nyasha about the grass, so vibrant now. The air around us smelled fresh with the scent of moist earth and life. Against the wall of the house, the rosebushes bloomed.

"It's like late spring or early summer back here," I said to Nyasha while I readied the phone for our next photo.

"I never would've guessed the rain could do this." He stared out over the lawn, and I also looked at the rich green blades with the crimson and gold leaves scattered over them. After a summer of yellow grass, our backyard had come to life just as the trees around us began to crawl inside themselves for another year.

Dry leaves crumbled beneath my feet, but the bright lawn called me to believe in miracles and comebacks and surprises. With the trees ablaze with fierce colors, framed by a dimming sky, I grasped a flash of glory, where the unexpected bursts forth and life pierces death. These were the moments I longed for, the single incidences that accumulate over a lifetime and speak of the world as it could be. Colors and patterns I witnessed on this day and then another day and another day, reminding me that my lungs filled with breath and I was alive. Maybe for this moment just before the sun sank below the horizon, before the chill of evening sent my family and me indoors—maybe I could hope for an abundance of impossible things?

I set the phone at the right angle and, after a pause, I nestled myself again within the border of my family.

The Saturday before Christmas, I drove Sekai to our church for the Christmas play rehearsal. The next day she would wear a white robe, and her shoulders would support wings. Beneath the golden lights of the sanctuary, her pale voice would glow with Christmas hymns.

This is a season that echoes with welcome. Strands of lights twisted around a stranger's home, an invitation to stop and gaze. Plates of molasses cookies delivered to the open arms of neighbors. Hearty meals shared with friends. And remembrance of a long-ago family offered shelter near a manger.

In church the next morning, sitting in an audience bulging with visitors, I would smile and greet those around me. Surrounded by the noise and song, my eyes would lift over the crowd and glance at the simple wooden cross hanging above the stage. Streaks of midmorning light from the windows would point to the world beyond. Then I would turn back to my row, offer bright smiles to the new faces, and remember how months ago, across the state border, others welcomed a stranger in their midst and paid for that good deed with their lives.

But the Saturday before Christmas, as on nearly every other day of the year, I headed toward the tall buildings of Charlotte. Sekai and I passed first the gas station and then the grocery store. A momentary gust shook bare tree branches and sent a couple of the few remaining leaves quivering into the air. That day the Confederate flag stretched taut in the sky, wind ripples coursing through the fabric.

I slowed my car and stared longer than usual at this object, this symbol, this thing I always searched to find. For the first time since the start of autumn, when I noticed the new flag with the white print, I could read the words.

"I ain't coming down," the message on the flag read. "I ain't coming down."

For months I had hoped for something that would never happen. Now that the leaves had fallen and the branches were empty, I could see clearly. My foot pressed against the gas and took my daughter and me away from this bit of road where I couldn't remain.

Minutes after I read the words on the flag, the song, "O Come All Ye Faithful," played on the radio. "Joyful and triumphant," I sang along and let my voice join with the voices on the radio and the choirs of unseen angels. When I sang the repeated words, "O come," my singing didn't grow in strength and certainty. Rather it softened to a near whisper.

The final verse began just before I merged the car onto the highway that moved me toward the center of Charlotte. Here my voice closed, and I listened to others sing familiar words with an intensity I couldn't muster. Then, with lanes of pummeling cars on each side of me, the music faded to quiet. Ahead of me the shiny buildings of the city awaited in the distance, but I ignored the metallic allure. Instead, I angled my car toward my exit, left the many lanes, and followed the curve of the narrow road.

Chapter 27

So That We Can Remember

Once, you brought home already-prepared hake coated in a golden-fried finish. The grease spread through the rough paper the deli worker used to contain your purchase, and the moisture from the hot fish dampened the inside of the grocery bag. In your other arm you carried a sack of white potatoes.

That was back when we were newly married, when we lived in Cape Town, when our first child had only just begun to form in my womb. "Fish and chips," I said to you that morning before you left for the office, leaving me alone in the solitude of our two-bedroom flat. "I'm desperate for fish and chips." All I could think about was the little fast-food restaurant in Anchorage where my mother used to take me as a child. They served steaming cups of clam chowder followed by baskets of battered cod and thick-cut fries.

That evening you stood in our doorway, perspiration beading at your hairline and trickling down the sides of your face—a familiar signature finish to your daily uphill walk from the nearest train station. Perhaps there was even more sweat that day with your detour to the grocery store.

"They were out of chips," you explained as you set the potatoes on our kitchen counter. Moments later you searched for the cutting board and found a sharp knife. One by one you held several potatoes beneath a stream of cold water, the heel of your hand rubbing off bits of dust and dirt. Then you pulled out the heavy cast-iron skillet from the cabinet by the stove. Occasionally you glanced at where I sat at the edge of the counter, swinging my legs back and forth. Each time you turned your head in my direction, you smiled.

You tell me that you don't remember that evening. You tell me how Cape Town feels like a millennium ago. I think you've forgotten how it felt to brush your lips against mine each morning and then walk down the long hill to wait for a packed train. I think you can't recall the heat of that summer, the way the air smelled as if a hint of ocean salt lingered around us. I think you can no longer hear the sounds of our neighborhood, the squeal of car and bus horns, the voices of people beginning their days.

What you remember is the way I wished for someone to talk with in your absence, the way I welcomed you home each evening with stories of the emptiness, the way I spoke in hiccupped dramatics and declared our unborn child to be my only friend. What you recollect is how I thumbed through photographs of Anchorage and how you wished that you and I could be us, but I could also be there.

There are many things we have chosen in life. We chose each other. We chose marriage. And in the beginning, before an engagement ring and wedding plans, we chose to believe that the approximately 10,500 miles that separated Anchorage from Cape Town, that separated me from you, were of little consequence. A plane ride or two or three. A dozen time zones. Nothing insurmountable.

You were unexpected to me. I was unexpected to you. We know these things now, and we laugh when we recall that day we met in the Cape Town airport. You speak of the rugby game you ended up having to miss in order to do your friend the favor of picking me up from the airport. I talk of the weariness I felt with each new beginning and how I wished I hadn't applied for the grant to go to Cape Town.

But there you were, standing next to our mutual friend. Your unfamiliar smile welcomed me to South Africa after my long journey from the other side of the world. Over a quick breakfast at the airport café, I learned how to pronounce your name and discovered that university studies had originally pulled you from your Zimbabwean homeland.

Ten weeks later we stood once more in the Cape Town airport. "You're making my life complicated," I said to you before you gave me a hug goodbye. True words, to be sure. And indeed, I was making your life complicated too.

Fifteen months after that, marriage was our choice. Walking together back down a grassy aisle strewn with red, pink, and white rose petals was our choice too. We never chose living in South Africa, though. What we did was pick a life where countries and cultures and—more important—messy administrative paperwork, like visa applications and work permits, became realities we juggled along with our vows.

Cape Town was a place for us to begin. The city where we met became our shared home. Not the change we wanted, but the only place that welcomed both of us promptly within its borders. In the absence of a South African work permit, I traded in a fledgling career in nonprofit management for long, quiet days in a new home. Lonely days too. Long, quiet, lonely days.

Fish and chips. All I could think about that particular morning in those early months of our marriage was the taste of flaky pieces of fish and savory grease on the tips of each of my fingers. And now you don't remember the weight of the potatoes or the way you poured vegetable oil into a hot pan. Now you look at me, and your eyes grow distant as if glancing over my shoulder to the faded past.

"I wish it had been different. I wish I could have changed it," you say.

I shake my head once and then again before I reply, "No." I remind you about those late nights I sat up in a curtain of dark with our newborn daughter cradled in my forearms. With my free hands I held that old iPod Touch and pecked out one word and then another. I formed paragraphs and turned snippets of thoughts into fleshed-out ideas. While you were at work and our daughter napped, I took my nighttime notes and shaped my first article. I submitted those words just before I took the laundry off the drying rack and folded bright new onesies alongside your graying gym socks.

"I emerged a writer," I tell you. In those fragile beginnings, that crucible produced a writer. I exchanged a fledgling career for a thing I couldn't have imagined. The aspirations of old found new life with a pen, a computer, and the blank lines of a notebook.

Now it's been over six years since we left Cape Town and moved to my country. We picked Charlotte, and we wagered that perhaps this city neither of us had been to before might be a good place for a new home. I want to say these years have been seamless and the move blessed our souls with a certain fullness, but I can't. In many ways we flounder, and I watch you do all you can to keep your head from sinking beneath unseen waves.

I look back to those first days here, when we navigated icy roads left over from a great winter storm. You told me that people didn't understand your accent. You said no one could pronounce your name. Though I recognize where we started and acknowledge the great distance we have come, I still feel far from the harmonious place I dream we will one day find. I continue to shape words and sentences and paragraphs, and I cling to a belief that this time is also a crucible where something unknown, unanticipated, and unimagined might emerge.

That day, closing in on a decade ago now—a millennium ago, you say—you turned the sack of potatoes you carried up a hill into thick-cut rectangles fit for a frying pan. We pulled two stools up to the counter. We ate pieces of grocery-store hake. We lifted hot chips to our mouths. A medley of reheated fish and cooling oil and wisps of fresh evening air swirled through our small home.

You looked at me, and I looked at you, and there was nowhere else for either of us to turn. We ate in semisilence with just a pepper of, "This is so good. Thank you so much," followed by, "You're welcome." The kitchen light cast a faint yellow across the walls and cushioned the room in a muted glow.

Acknowledgments

In no way did I write this book in isolation even if the act of writing may—at times—happen in solitude. To anyone who considers themselves a positive part of my life in big or small ways, I thank you for your words of encouragement, your prayers, your interest in my work, your love for me and my family, your reminder that I'm part of something greater than myself, and so much more.

Thank you to the many editors who have seen the value of my writing. Thank you especially to the editors of the publications where some of these essays originally appeared.

Thank you to my amazing agent, Lisa Jackson, for finding me and dreaming with me about the possibilities. Sometimes the very thing people say never happens actually does, and I write these words with deep gratitude. Thank you to my editors, Megan Dobson and Debbie Wickwire, and really everyone at W Publishing. I've felt buoyed by your excitement about this book, and I'm honored to be part of a team that believes in the importance of these words.

Thank you to the Arts & Science Council of Charlotte-Mecklenburg County, the North Carolina Arts Council, Writers & Books, GrubStreet, the *Image Journal* Glen Workshop, and the Collegeville Institute for the generous support that helped make this book possible and helped me become the writer that I am. Thank you, CharlotteLit, for serving me and other writers in my community.

Thank you to my Charlotte-based writing group and my virtual writing group for your critique and praise. Your insights have made me a better writer. Thank you to my many wonderful teachers who saw potential and pushed me forward, especially Lisa Ohlen Harris.

Thank you to my CMU ladies—Sherae Daniel, Zalenda Cyrille, Nina Jackson, and Jaime Johnson. Over two decades of friendship, and the word *grateful* feels insufficient. Thank you to LaTonya Archibald, Denise Flanders, Kate Motaung, Patty B. Griesemer, Lindsay and Ryan Rich, and LisaNoelle and Mawethu Ncaca. Your ongoing excitement, prayers, and encouragement have sustained me through the joys and the struggles of this unexpected journey.

Much gratitude to all those who read essay drafts and/or talked with me about the ideas that became the beginnings of many of these essays. These words are better because of the input of so many of you. Thank you to Nina Jackson and Melanie Best for reading the entire manuscript with an eye for sensitivity.

Thank you to all the cities, states, and countries I've ever called even a temporary home—but particularly to Alaska where I'm from and North Carolina where I now live. I write with a richness because of both.

Thank you to Ellah Gopo and Nyengeterai Gopo for the way you warmly welcomed me into your family. Thank you to my parents, Shirley Harduar and Tony Harduar, for the family we were and the faith you gave me. I'm blessed with the memories of my childhood and the love of my parents. Thank you to my sister, Laurel Harduar-Morano, who has shared much of this journey with me and is my first friend. To both you and Aaron, we'll always have the sweet memories of Chapel Hill.

To my daughters, my Laughter and my Miracle, words of thanks are not enough to express the happiness you both bring me. Watching you grow gives me hope because you begin better than me and better than my generation. May your mother's journey offer you courage for your own.

And Nyasha, my love. I dedicate this book to you, but I also thank you for the way you believed in my writing long before I ever could, long before there was much to believe in. The secret to all of this was finding you. This side of heaven, I am home with you.

Finally, thank you to Jesus Christ, my Lord, my Savior, my God. This is a life I could not have imagined, and it is my hope and desire to use this life to honor you.

Notes

Chapter 1: Heaven's Boxes
1. Genesis 15:5 NASB.

Chapter 2: Earth's Freckled Sky
1. Genesis 1:1.

Chapter 3: A Theory of Known Elements
1. "Jamaica: History," Lonely Planet, accessed November 27, 2017, https://www.lonelyplanet.com/jamaica/history.
2. "Did You Know?" Alaska Conservation Foundation (website), accessed November 27, 2017, https://alaskaconservation.org/experience-alaska/did-you-know/.

Chapter 6: Acts of Cleaving
1. Genesis 2:24 KJV.
2. *Merriam-Webster*, s.v. "cleave" (v.), accessed November 27, 2017, https://www.merriam-webster.com/dictionary/cleave.
3. "Gore's Eldest Daughter Weds New York Doctor in Washington," All Politics: CNN.com, July 12, 1997, http://www.cnn.com/ALLPOLITICS/1997/07/12/gore.wedding/.
4. Huma Khan, "Gores' Eldest Daughter Karenna

Separates from Husband of 12 Years," ABC News.com, June 9, 2010, http://abcnews.go.com/Politics/Media/karenna-gore-schiff-daughter-al-tipper-gore-separates/story?id=10867670.

5. Jean-Baptiste Thiebot et. al., "Mates but Not Sexes Differ in Migratory Niche in a Monogamous Penguin Species," *Biology Letters*, The Royal Society Publishing, September 9, 2015, http://rsbl.royalsocietypublishing.org/content/roybiolett/11/9/20150429.full.pdf.

Chapter 8: Washing Dishes in the Family of God

1. Luke 14:8, 10.
2. Philippians 2:5 NLT, paraphrased.
3. Philippians 2:7, paraphrased.

Chapter 10: Notes on the Hair Spectrum

1. "Types of Relaxers," Design Essentials, accessed December 26, 2017, http://designessentials.com/types-of-relaxers/.
2. "Garrett Morgan," Biography.com, last modified February 2, 2016, https://www.biography.com/people/garrett-morgan-9414691.
3. Henry Louis Gates Jr., "High Cheekbones and Straight Black Hair?" *The Root*, December 29, 2014, http://www.theroot.com/high-cheekbones-and-straight-black-hair-1790878167.
4. Lydia Polgreen, "For Mixed-Race South Africans, Equity Is Elusive," *New York Times*, July 27, 2003, http://www.nytimes.com/2003/07/27/world/for-mixed-race-south-africans-equity-is-elusive.html.
5. "Hair Types," Naturally Curly, accessed November 29, 2017, https://www.naturallycurly.com/hair-types.
6. Gates, "High Cheekbones and Straight Black Hair?"

Chapter 12: Role Model, or Black Girls May Have Dreamed of Engineering Because of Women Like Me

1. National Science Foundation, National Center for Science and Engineering Statistics, "Science and Engineering Bachelor's Degrees Earned by Black or African American women, by Field: 1995–2014,"

in *Women, Minorities, and Persons with Disabilities in Science and Engineering: 2017*, Special Report NSF 17-310, available at https://www.nsf.gov/statistics/2017/nsf17310/digest/fod-wmreg/black-women-by-field.cfm.

2. Trina Fletcher, Monique Ross, DeLean Tolbert, James Holly, Monica Cardella, Allison Godwin, and Jennifer DeBoer, "Ignored Potential: A Collaborative Road Map for Increasing African American Women in Engineering" (White Paper, Purdue University, 2017), 3.

Chapter 13: On Degrees of Blackness and Being Me

1. Lerone Bennett Jr., "What's In a Name?" *Ebony*, November 1967, http://www.virginia.edu/woodson/courses/aas102%20(spring%2001)/articles/names/bennett.htm; "African American, (the Term); A Brief History," African American Registry, accessed November 29, 2017, https://aaregistry.org/story/african-american-the-term-a-brief-history/.

2. Mary C. Waters, *Black Identities: West Indian Immigrant Dreams and American Realities* (Cambridge, Massachusetts: Harvard University Press, 2001), 45.

3. Vinay Harpalani, "DesiCrit: Theorizing the Racial Ambiguity of South Asian Americans," *New York University Annual Survey of American Law* 69, no. 1 (2013): 134–35.

4. United States Department of Commerce, Bureau of the Census, "Sixteenth Census of the United States: 1940, Population Schedule," PDF available at Census.gov (website), accessed November 29, 2017, https://www.census.gov/history/pdf/1940_population_questionnaire.pdf.

5. Bureau of the Census, "1980 Census Short Form," PDF available at Census.gov (website), accessed November 29, 2017, https://www.census.gov/history/pdf/1980_short_questionnaire.pdf.

6. Bureau of the Census, "1970 Census Questionnaire," PDF available at Census.gov, accessed November 29, 2017, https://www.census.gov/history/pdf/1970_questionnaire.pdf.

7. Bureau of the Census, "2000 Census Short Form," accessed November 29, 2017, https://www.census.gov/history/pdf/2000_short_form.pdf.

8. Campbell Gibson and Kay Jung, "Historical Census Statistics on

the Foreign-Born Population of the United States: 1850 to 2000," Working Paper No. 81, Population Division, U.S. Census Bureau, 2006, 41, https://www.census.gov/population/www/documentation/twps0081/twps0081.pdf.

9. "U.S. Immigration Since 1965," History.com, 2010, accessed November 29, 2017, http://www.history.com/topics/us-immigration-since-1965.

10. Gibson and Jung, "Historical Census Statistics on the Foreign-Born Population," 41.

Chapter 14: Recalling What Was Good

1. John Turner and Geoffrey Parson, "Oh! My Pa-Pa" (English lyrics). Original German version of this song, "Oh mein Papa" written by Paul Burkhard, 1939. Recorded by Eddie Fisher with Hugo Winterhalter's orchestra and chorus, December 12, 1953.

Chapter 15: Plucked and Planted

1. Ta-Nehisi Coates, "My President Was Black," *Atlantic*, January– February 2017, https://www.theatlantic.com/magazine/archive/2017/01/my-president-was-black/508793/.

2. Royal Botanic Gardens, *Kew Science: Plants of the World Online*, s.v. "*Musa balbisiana* Colla," accessed December 1, 2017, http://powo.science.kew.org/taxon/urn:lsid:ipni.org:names:797536-1.

Chapter 16: A Lingering Thread

1. Rebecca Tortello, "Out Of Many Cultures, the People Who Came: The Arrival of the Indians," Jamaica Gleaner, November 3, 2003, http://old.jamaica-gleaner.com/pages/history/story0057.htm.

2. Pico Iyer, "Where Is Home?" filmed June 2013 at TEDGlobal 2013 Think Again conference, Edinburgh, Scotland, TED video, 14:01, https://www.ted.com/talks/pico_iyer_where_is_home/details.

3. Henry Louis Gates Jr., writer, director, and narrator, *African American Lives*, DVD (PBS Home Video, 2006).

Chapter 18: Marking the Color Trail

1. Uri Friedman, "How an Ad Campaign Invented the Diamond Engagement Ring," *Atlantic*, February 13, 2015, https://www.theatlantic.com/international/archive/2015/02/how-an-ad-campaign-invented-the-diamond-engagement-ring/385376/.

2. Madeleine Luckel, "Queen Victoria Made White Wedding Dresses Popular. Here's What Else You Should Know About Her Royal Wedding," *Vogue*, January 15, 2017, http://www.vogue.com/article/queen-victoria-royal-wedding-facts-victoria-premiere; "Queen Victoria's Wedding Lace," Textile Research Centre, last modified September 11, 2016, http://trc-leiden.nl/trc-needles/clothing-undergarment/individual-textiles-and-textile-types/secular-ceremonies-and-rituals/queen-victorias-wedding-lace.

Chapter 24: Marching Toward Zion

1. Martin Luther King Jr., "Paul's Letter to American Christians," sermon given at Dexter Avenue Baptist Church, Montgomery, AL, November 4, 1956, *King Institute Encyclopedia*, documents section, accessed December 2, 2017, http://kingencyclopedia.stanford.edu/encyclopedia/documentsentry/doc_pauls_letter_to_american_christians.1.html.

2. Galatians 3:28.

3. Christopher P. Scheitle and Kevin D. Dougherty, "Race, Diversity, and Membership Duration in Religious Congregations," *Sociological Inquiry* 80, no. 3 (2010): 405–423, https://doi.org//10.1111/j.1475-682X.2010.00340.x.

Chapter 26: An Abundance of Impossible Things

1. Reuven Blau, Sasha Goldstein, and Corky Siemaszko, "Remembering the Victims: Stories of 9 Killed in Charleston," *New York Daily News*, last modified June 19, 2015, http://www.nydailynews.com/news/national/victims-charleston-church-shooting-diverse-group-article-1.2263187.

2. Michael Gordon and Bruce Henderson, "Charleston Shooting Suspect

Captured in Shelby," *Charlotte Observer*, June 18, 2015, http://www.charlotteobserver.com/news/local/article24863200.html.

3. Jennifer Olsen Kelley and J. Lawrence Angel, "Life Stresses of Slavery," *American Journal of Physical Anthropology* 74 (1987): 199–211.

About the Author

Patrice Gopo is the daughter of Jamaican immigrants, and she was born and raised in Anchorage, Alaska. Her essays have appeared in a variety of literary journals and other publications, including *Creative Nonfiction*, *Gulf Coast*, and *Christianity Today*. Her radio commentaries have been featured on her local public radio station. Her writing has been nominated for a Pushcart Prize, and she is the grateful recipient of a North Carolina Arts Council Fellowship in Literature.

Patrice has a bachelor of science in chemical engineering from Carnegie Mellon University and both a master of business administration and a master of public policy from the University of Michigan. While she is thankful she's had the opportunity to study several different subjects, she's also thrilled that engineering led to community development, which led to writing. Sometimes she wonders what might be next. She lives with her family in North Carolina—a place she has recently begun to consider another home.

Please visit her website at patricegopo.com.